In Search of Brazil's Quantum Surgeon

The Dr. Fritz Phenomenon

By Masao Maki

Cadence Books • San Francisco

Translated by Masao Maki with the assistance of Denny Townsend

Editor-in-Chief/Satoru Fujii
Cover Design/Ted Szeto
Publisher/Seiji Horibuchi

Original copyright 1997 Masao Maki
Translation copyright 1998 Masao Maki and Cadence Books
All rights reserved

Printed in Canada
ISBN 1-56931-297-4
First Printing, October 1998

Cadence Books
A division of Viz Communications, Inc.
A subsidiary of Shogakukan, Inc.
P.O. Box 77010
San Francisco, CA 94107

CONTENTS

The original Dr. Fritz, a German army surgeon who died in the first World War

In order to cure a baby, Dr. Fritz operates on its healthy mother.

Dr. Moura measured Dr. Fritz's brain waves.

An amazing Umbanda healer from Baixinha

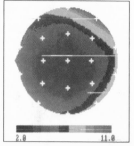

Dr. Fritz's brain waves are measured on nineteen points. Incredibly, all were above forty hertz.

David and Anna Sonnenschein in Cesarina's stately mansion

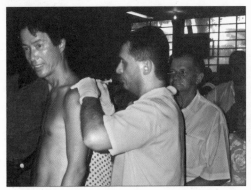

Author Maki and his travel partner Kaori have collaborated on two books which debunked supernatural phenomenon in India and Peru.

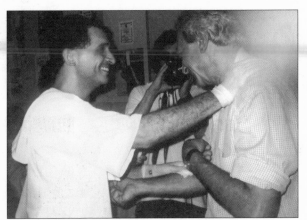

Dr. Fritz said, "Pleas focus on my hand. You will get pictures of light coming in."

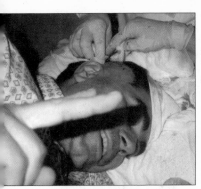

A patient jokes with the author during brain surgery, without anesthesia, to remove a tumor.

Due to his astigmatism, Rubens is myopic, but when he channels Dr. Fritz, he can see without eyeglasses.

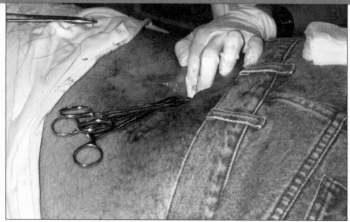
Dr. Fritz rejuvenates bones by manipulating this patient's electromagnetic field.

Kinko Sensei, São Paulo's Shinto priestess

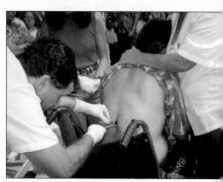
A very quick herniated disk surgery with no anesthesia, no pain, and no blood

Dr. Fritz single-handedly treats 1,000 patients a day.

The moment when computer engineer Rubens channels the spirit of Dr. Fritz

A woman walking home immediately following cancer surgery

The author interviews Ram Dass.

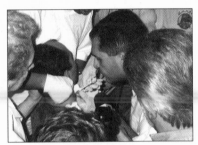

This patient continued talking and smiling as Dr. Fritz removed a bullet from his neck.

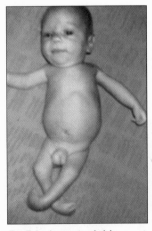

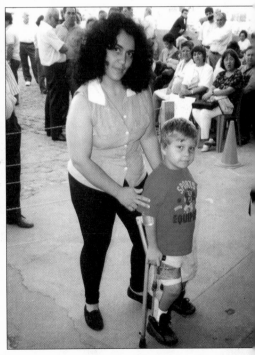

Dr. Fritz improved this boy's polio symptoms dramatically with an astral-body injection. Compare his photo as an infant to the one on the right.

Foreword

By Stanley Krippner, Ph.D.

One of the most celebrated healers of modern times was Zé Arigó, a Brazilian farmer who claimed to incorporate the spirit of Dr. Fritz, a German physician who supposedly died during the First World War. Arigó died in 1971, but Dr. Fritz has reappeared since, almost always as a healer, but once as a politician. (However, the candidate who claimed to have incorporated the spirit of Dr. Fritz lost the election!)

In 1985, I met someone who claimed to have Dr. Fritz's alleged healing power, Edson Cavalcante de Queiroz, an obstetrician and gynecologist working in Recife, Brazil. We were both attending a conference in Sao Paulo, and Queiroz agreed to conduct a private session, during which he worked with half a dozen volunteers. As he sliced flesh with a scalpel and gave injections with surgical needles, I noticed a curious phenomenon. All three of the volunteers from the United States winced or screamed with pain, while the Brazilian volunteers were silent and stoic. Upon reflection, I realized that the Brazilians knew of Dr. Fritz's reputation as a painless practitioner, whereas the Americans had no such preconception. The expectation with which one enters a healing session is bound to affect one's response, whether the practitioner is an allopathic physician, a Spiritist "channeler," or—as was the case with Queiroz—both.

Edson Queiroz was killed by an associate in 1991 after a business deal went sour. Even before his death, Rubens Faria, a computer engineer living in Rio de Janeiro, contended that he was "channeling" Dr. Fritz as well. In addition, in 1993, when I led a tour group to Brazil, I met Mauricio Magalhaes, who *also* claimed to be "channeling" Dr. Fritz. During a lengthy session in a private home, "Dr. Fritz" favored us with his presence, and a few members of our group volunteered for treatment. I had prepared them in advance for the experience, telling them that Dr. Fritz was renowned for operating with a minimum of pain; happily, their experiences conformed to this expectation!

An American anthropologist, Sidney Greenfield, interviewed thirty-two of Magalhaes's clients. During Greenfield's interviews, each of which lasted about ninety minutes, he asked eighteen questions. Only 14% of the clients said they experienced pain, despite the lack of anesthetics, and even though all but one said they had been subjected to the insertion of needles or incision with a scalpel. Only one of the respondents claimed to have experienced complications, 88% claimed to have been helped by the treatment, and 64% pronounced that they had been "cured" of their ailment. Of the thirty-two clients, 95% said they preferred Magalhaes to conventional medical treatment. When asked if their experience had influenced their point of view about religion, 56% answered that they were now more positively inclined toward the Spiritist faiths. These faiths have proliferated in Brazil since colonial times, due in part to the arrival of African slaves who continued their native practices, many of which involved spirit incorporation.

When I write about the Dr. Fritz phenomenon or discuss it at psychological conferences, I use the adjective "dissociative" to describe it. For me, the term "dissociative" can be applied to reported experiences and observed behaviors that seem to exist apart from, or appear to be disconnected from, the mainstream, or flow, of one's conscious awareness, behavioral repertoire, and/or self-identity. "Dissociation" is a noun used to describe a person's involvement in these reported "dissociative" experiences or to describe observed "dissociative" behaviors.

I apply the word "dissociative" to phenomenological reports and behavioral observations that pertain to personal concepts and memories. Individuals harbor several identities, as well as a multiplicity of memories covering their behavior, affect, sensations, and knowledge. When these constellations become disconnected, the result can be described as "dissociation." One example of dissociation would be ruptures in concepts of self-identity; another would be gaps in memories about events occurring in a particular time and place. In instances of "dissociative identity disorder," an individual has several identities (or "multiple personalities") that are out of control. The typical result of this condition, which I consider to be extremely rare, is distress, misery, and torment. Fortunately, there are some skilled psychotherapists (another rare breed) who can help the afflicted individual mold these shattered pieces into a coherent whole.

Dissociative identity disorder represents uncontrolled dissociation. The "channeling" of Dr. Fritz qualifies as an example of dissociation because there is a major shift in the "channeler's" self-identity. However, the Dr. Fritz phenomenon is marked by control and by the positive utilization of this condition. Another extraordinary example of controlled dissociation came to my attention during a 1971 visit to Brazil, when I heard of Francisco Candido "Chico" Xavier. Born in 1910, Xavier reported his first experience with automatic writing in 1927 and completed his first "channeled" book in 1932. This was followed by over 300 other books purportedly "written" by some 600 "spirits" for whom Xavier served as a "medium" or "control." Besides poetry, the "dictated" material consists of historical romances, fiction, essays, plays, and moral teachings. These books have sold over 18 million copies in Brazil and have been translated into three dozen languages, and Xavier has donated all the profit from sales to charity. In these instances, there were numerous displacements of Xavier's self-identity.

A fairly consistent similarity among the Brazilian "channelers" and mediums whom I have observed is their purported inability to recall the events of the incorporation after the "spirits" have departed. However, this amnesiac quality can just as easily be explained as an "achievement"; each failure to remember adds legitimacy to a medium's reputation. In other words, I interpret this type of controlled dissociation as a goal-directed activity, and find this concept helpful in understanding the phenomenon of Dr.

Fritz and other types of mediumship.

Arigó, Queiroz, Magalhaes, Faria, and others who claim to have incorporated Dr. Fritz insist that they do not remember the events that occur once he has made his appearance. This amnesia is thought to demonstrate the authenticity of both Dr. Fritz and the incorporation experience. On the other hand, I have also observed indigenous shamans who reportedly allow "spirits" to use their bodies as vehicles to receive various messages and to conduct healing work; in these cases, amnesia is rare—but shamans and mediums are two very different types of practitioners, the former taking pride in their control and the latter in their passivity.

In 1996, I met Masao Maki at an international transpersonal psychology conference in Manaus, Brazil. I had been to Manaus on two previous visits and to Brazil more than a dozen times. But for novices like Maki, Brazil is an exotic country, and the banks of the Amazon River were an exemplary location for the conference. Maki was fascinated by Brazil and its wonders, and took a special interest in the Dr. Fritz phenomenon. At the same conference, I encountered a young friend of mine hobbling about with a cane as a result of a drastic accident that had occurred while rock climbing some years earlier. He returned to the United States a few weeks later without his cane, maintaining that he had been the beneficiary of Dr. Fritz's ministrations during a detour to Rio.

My only regret is that so little medical research has been done on the Dr. Fritz phenomenon. Dr. Garfield's article on Dr. Fritz was published in 1997. In 1996, the Brazilian psychologist Dr. Margarida de Carvalho published a case study of a Brazilian dancer whom she accompanied to Palmello, Brazil, where they visited a practitioner who claimed to incorporate "Dr. Ricardo," another German "spirit doctor." Garfield's article is a model of a long-term investigation of an entire group, whereas Dr. de Carvalho's article is the prototype of an in-depth case study in which a successful healing was claimed from which the benefits were still evident after one year.

Do these "spirit doctors" represent discarnate entities returning to earth in order to complete their healing mission? Are they archetypal forces from the collective unconscious? Are they sub-personalities, fantasies, or downright fabrications? Only time—and disciplined investigation—will tell. In the meantime, the curious reader can do no better than to read Masao Maki's memoir, *In Search of Brazil's Quantum Surgeon*. Maki is a delightful storyteller, and the tales he tells demonstrate over and over that Western medicine has not closed its accounts with reality.

MESSENGER FROM AN ANGEL

May 12, 1996

I had some time to spare before my midnight flight to South America departed, so I decided to stop by the duty-free shop in the international waiting room at Miami Airport. As I browsed, I noticed a middle-aged Caucasian woman wearing a pure white Indian dress, a short distance from me. She was watching me, and when I looked at her, she smiled, her bright white teeth flashing.

A moment later she came over and asked, in a husky voice, "Hi. Where are you going this time?" I was a little surprised, but I answered, "I'm going to Brazil on the midnight flight." Her green eyes shone as she said, "Oh yeah? So you're going to meet Dr. Fritz, eh?"

What was this strange lady talking about? I almost dismissed her with a laugh, but something told me she wasn't just kidding around, so I told her, "No, I'm going to the International Transpersonal Psychology Conference at Manaus. But who is this Dr. What's-his-name?"

"His name is Dr. Fritz. He's going to cure Superman." Her voice was brimming with confidence.

"What? Superman?"

"Oh yes, Superman. You know, Christopher Reeve, the actor who had the horseback-riding accident?"

I didn't know what to say. Just then her friends came to the door of the shop to fetch her. She waved to them, then turned and hugged me very tightly. As she did so, she whispered in my ear, tickling it with her lips, "I feel pretty sure you're going to meet Dr. Fritz." Then she gazed into my eyes for a moment, turned, and walked towards her waiting friends.

Standing there watching her retreating figure, I thought, "Déjà vu. It's happened again." You see, last year, en route to Mexico, I had had a similar experience at the Dallas airport. I was also killing time at the duty-free shop when a strange lady approached me and asked, "Where are you going?" I didn't answer, because I assumed she wanted to sell me something, and moved to the other side of the shop to avoid her. Then the store clerk came over and asked, "Where are you going?" Again I was reluctant to answer, but I said, "I'm going to Puerto Vallarta." His expression changed and he said, "Oh, your plane left four minutes ago."

Suddenly I realized there was a one-hour difference between Texas and Colorado and that I had failed to reset my watch. In a panic, I ran to the gate and got there just in time to make the flight, just as the gate was closing. Once I was safely on board and had a moment to think about it, I concluded that some sort of guardian angel had spoken to me through the woman and the clerk at the duty-free shop. My angel had used them to send me the message to hurry up.

Now, a year later, this strange woman I had just met seemed to be yet another messenger. I felt a thrill of anticipation, as if something unexpected was going to happen on this journey.

I considered her words: "I feel pretty sure that you are going to meet Dr. Fritz." But there must be hundreds of thousands of doctors in Brazil, so how would I find this particular Dr. Fritz? Healing Superman? That sounded pretty cheesy, pretty fishy, to me. And "Dr. Fritz" didn't even sound like a Brazilian name; it sounded German. The only Fritz I had ever heard of was the professional wrestler Fritz Von Eric, who was famous when I was a kid. I began fondly reminiscing about the good old days when professional wrestlers had names like Biting Fred Brassy, the Iron Claw, the Destroyer, Mr. X, and the Sharp Brothers, and it was hard for me to take this other "Fritz" seriously.

December 21, 2012:
The Day of Time Wave Zero

May 13

Whew! The trip from Denver to São Paulo via Miami took more than twenty hours, including waiting time at airports.

When I finally arrived, I gazed at the high ceiling in the São Paulo airport and sighed. Half jokingly, I said, "God, this is too much for me! Please give me a break!" But when I boarded the jumbo jet to Manaus, the flight attendant guided me toward the first-class section on the second floor. At first, I couldn't believe my good fortune. Since I only had an economy-class ticket, I muttered to myself, "They must be making a mistake." But when the flight took off and no one came to escort me back downstairs to the cheaper seats, I concluded that the economy section must be full.

Remembering my little prayer in the airport, I thought perhaps I had been granted a wish by the genie of a magic lamp. Had I misused the wish to get me this huge first-class seat? "Oh well," I thought, "this is the first time I've ever had a taste of luxury like this. Maybe once in a lifetime is all right." I looked around the space, which could be described as the jumbo jet's forehead. It was like the plush living room of the super-rich and famous. A very attractive flight attendant brought me a real crystal glass filled with expensive, delicious wine. I hadn't slept much on the previous flights, so before I knew it, I was pretty drunk.

In this dreamy state, I decided to read the itinerary for my trip to Brazil. Until that moment, I had been too busy to examine it carefully. It was only the week before that I decided to go. But when I saw my schedule following the conference in Manaus, I began to sober up quickly. I couldn't find any mention of a tour of Brazil. I was certain I had asked my travel agents to include a tour of cities such as Brasília, the famous city of the future; Recife, the Venice of Brazil; and Salvador, the Rome of Brazil's blacks. Then I realized that the date of my return flight to the United States conflicted with such tours. As I read on, I discovered to my horror that I was going to be in Rio de Janeiro for nine days without hotel reservations. I had heard Rio de Janeiro was an unsafe city filled with slums and had read newspaper accounts about Rio's police hunting down and killing homeless children. I cursed the tour company and I cursed myself for forgetting to confirm my after-conference travel plans.

Deeply disappointed, I thought, "What am I going to do in this dangerous city for nine days?" To calm myself, I began thinking about how I could compromise. Maybe I could just stay safely ensconced in the hotel and work on the manuscript for my debut book in English, *Spiritual Adventures of a Sushi Chef*.

As these contingency plans passed through my mind, I glanced out the window at the deep green of the Amazon rain forest below us. I remembered that someone had called it the "lungs of the planet," because its lush green leaves breathe in the world's carbon dioxide and exhale fresh oxygen for us to breathe. If it weren't for this huge oxygen factory, the world probably would have choked on its own fetid breath by now. I could see the ribbon of the Amazon, the world's largest river, home to more than 2,000 species of freshwater fish, and I pondered the concept of Gaia, the belief that Earth is a living organism. This place was like the metabolic center of the planet. My fears about the aftermath of the conference began to dissolve in my excitement about coming to the heart of this ecological wonderland, Manaus.

May 14

The Amazon River is so huge that a journey to the opposite shore by boat seems to take forever. One-sixth of the fresh water of the planet flows in this mighty river. The five-star Tropical

Hotel Manaus is situated on its shore. This was where the pre-conference workshop took place.

My roommate was a Canadian psychologist named Richard. Although he was seventy-six years old, he was full of energy and enthusiasm. I found him to be a fine example of someone who had achieved a lot of personal growth through psychotherapy and the Human Potential Movement. When I awoke on the first morning, Richard had already been swimming and was arranging his blond toupee in front of the room's large mirror.

My main purpose for coming to Brazil was to attend a workshop given by Don Manuel, a Q'ero Indian who lives in a village in the Andes mountains of Peru, 5,000 meters above sea level. He is a shaman and a direct descendant of the ancient Incas. My first encounter with him was not a dramatic one. Inside the hotel's workshop room, I saw, in the midst of some forty participants, one small, poor-looking old man seated on a metal folding chair. This was Don Manuel. I was reminded of a story I once heard about a beggar, perhaps a Tibetan. The beggar did nothing but smoke cigarettes in a corner of a bazaar, a vegetable market, but he was said to be far closer to Buddha than the high priests of the biggest temples. So I thought perhaps this unremarkable little man, Don Manuel, might be similar.

I wasn't disappointed. When he started the ceremony called Despachos, an offering to the spirits, his face changed dramatically. He was full of life, and the energy emanating from his small body more than filled the cavernous room. I was impressed.

Don Manuel is a fourth-level shaman, the highest level a shaman can attain. From him I learned the meditation technique called *Hoocha*. This technique is very effective in countering bad intentions or envy others may have towards you. *Hoocha* is a word for the vibrations of heavy energy, the negative thoughts, others direct toward you. Don Manuel explained that in the Inca way of thinking, there is no good or bad energy, only light or heavy energy, and in human beings, the spiritual digestive organ able to process these energies is located near the navel. In the Quechua language, the navel is called *cuzco*. Thus Cuzco, the ancient capital of the

Incas, was considered the navel energy center of the planet.

In Hoocha meditation, one begins by inhaling deeply into the abdomen, then imagines heavy energy being taken into the cuzco, the spiritual digestive organ near the navel. One visualizes biting and chewing that energy, digesting only the useful pure light energy within, called "sami." Then, as one exhales deeply, the leftover undigested energy is given back to the *Pachamama*, or Mother Earth, through both legs. Pachamama is believed to have the ability to digest or take in hoocha energy and return it as sami to the surface of the planet, much as tree leaves convert carbon dioxide to oxygen. Practice and mastery of this simple Hoocha meditation technique enables practitioners to love anyone, even people they dislike, because the negative energies are digested and used to become more energetic and powerful.

I really took this technique to heart and began using it constantly. I even bought T-shirts imprinted with the words "I eat Hoocha." I decided that even if all I learned was this technique, it was worth my expense in coming here. But Don Manuel surprised me with yet another teaching: the prophecy of the ancient Incas. We participants were honored to hear this prophecy, since until recently it had been forbidden knowledge to outsiders.

Five hundred years ago, the Q'ero tribe was driven out of Cuzco by invading Spaniards. In order to keep this ancient Inca prophecy secret, they hid themselves, living secretly on a high mountain where no Spanish influence could reach them. From generation to generation, this is the message that was passed down: In the future, when the number of condors decreased and the light of the sun changed, the Q'ero must descend from their mountain into the villages below and disseminate their knowledge throughout the world. About thirty years ago, these shamans learned that the number of condors had dropped dramatically, due to changes in the planet's eco-system, and that the color and appearance of the sun had changed because of the destruction of the planet's ozone layer. Realizing that the time had come, they began telling their story to the villagers in the foothills.

In 1949, a group of anthropologists discovered the Q'ero

Indians and their shamans. Don Manuel told us that, according to Inca prophecy, the years 1990 to 1993 were called the *Pachakuti*, the cosmic transmutation, a time during which preparations were made for the coming of a new era, of cosmic reordering. Then, in 1993, the world entered the initial nineteen-year phase of the *Taripay Pacha*, the era of "Meeting Ourselves Again." During this period, 1993 to 2012, the challenge for humanity is to sufficiently cleanse our collective energy bubble and draw down enough spiritual energy from *Hanaq Pacha*, or heaven, to collectively pass through the fourth-level initiation.

In Andean tradition, fourth-level shamans are those who can utilize universal energy and live with God. Don Juan Nunez del Prado, a professor of anthropology at Cuzco University, is also a twenty-eight-year disciple of Don Manuel. He told me that the Andean shamans are working extremely hard to try to manifest these prophecies. His hope is that people in other countries will also work on their spiritual development, so that they can contribute to the collective evolutionary shift.

So the question is, What will happen in 2012? Will there be an ascension of human consciousness, as many channelers are predicting, or will the world end in a great apocalypse, in Armageddon?

Something that surprised me: The year the Incas prophecy will usher in great change, 2012, coincides with the beginning of a new great cycle on the Mayan calendar of ancient Mexico. Furthermore, the year 2012 also coincides with a novel situation in Earth's history: the value of zero, according to the Time Wave Zero theory of Terence McKenna. I met Terence at a friend's party in Boulder. He explained his Time Wave Zero theory with his computer. Inspired by the sixty-four pictograms of the *I Ching*, he discovered that time is not smooth; rather, it has the structure of fractal movement. Based on this discovery, and using very complicated calculations, he has created a model of the oscillatory character of history. His model predicts all the historical events, from the fall of Rome to the European enlightenment to the end of World War II. According to the theory of Time Wave Zero, time is becoming more and more dense, and after December 21, 2012, it is going to become zero for the first time in planetary history. Around that day, he assumes that the most extraordinary event in the planet's history will occur.

Basically, I'm not an airy-fairy, wishy-washy New Ager who believes in such things as Nostradamus's prophecies or many of the other far-out theories propagated by channelers. But I was shocked to find that three different sources—the Incas, the Mayans, and Time Wave Zero—all indicate December of 2012 as the time of the greatest change in Earth and human history.

My conclusion, however, is that we don't need to be paranoid about the end of the world—but neither should we consider all these prophecies bogus. Rather, I think it would be beneficial for us to consider the possibility of human evolution, and for each of us to work on ourselves to become better people.

THE PSYCHEDELIC
CONFERENCE IN THE AMAZON

May 17

It was the first of six days at the International Transpersonal Psychology Conference at Tropical Hotel Manaus. I was told there were 800 participants from thirty-eight countries in attendance, mostly doctors, professors, and New Age intellectuals.

The conference began in the early morning with yoga and Tai Chi Chuan exercises. These were followed by two morning sessions, each divided into three tracks, with seminar titles such as "Shamanic Healing" and "Quantum Physics and the New Bio-Psycho-Physical Parallelism." In the afternoon, there were two more sessions with three tracks, including special tracks on transpersonal education and the therapeutic use of psychedelics. After dinner, we were treated to spiritual entertainment, with cultural performances by guest artists. The theme of the conference was "Technology of the Sacred." Exposed to such rich, intense programming, I felt certain I would be enlightened by the time the conference ended!

At the opening ceremonies, Dr. Stanislav Grof, a psychologist and the founding president of the International Transpersonal Association, gave the keynote address. The Rio Negro Hall was packed, and crackling with an air of expectation.

Dr. Grof spoke at length about the rich and versatile world of the spirit in Brazil, giving examples from some very active mystical cults, such as Umbanda and Candomblé. He explained that Brazil's indigenous people originally had their own shamans.

Then, with the invasion of the Spaniards and other European colonists, Catholicism was introduced. When black African slaves arrived, they brought with them their own spiritual traditions as well. At the end of the nineteenth century, Kardecist Spiritism, a practice based on the writings of Allan Kardec, a Frenchman, was introduced, and spread rapidly throughout the culture. Each religion influenced the other, and this mix was now bringing about a spiritual flowering in this South American nation. People call Brazil "the country where God is still breathing," Dr. Grof said. In Brazil, ninety percent of the people believe in the existence of spirit and God. Some psychologists say that most Brazilians are channelers.

At the end of his address, Dr. Grof said something that really caught my attention: "Currently, a young Brazilian computer programmer is channeling the spirit of a German doctor who died in World War I. He is treating thousands of patients and has an incredible success ratio." The 800 or so people gathered in Rio Negro Hall had, up until that moment, been listening very attentively and quietly, but as soon as Dr. Grof mentioned this channeler, many in the audience became agitated and expressed their skepticism aloud.

I wondered to myself, "Was this a mistake, telling such a far-out story to a highly educated crowd of academics?" But Dr. Grof maintained his calm, waited for the noise to subside, and then persevered. "In 1947," he continued, "an uneducated Brazilian farmer by the name of Zé Arigó was the first to incorporate the spirit of this German doctor. Overnight, Arigó began speaking German, a language he had never learned, and began performing operations on patients, using only a rusty knife, a pair of scissors, and no anesthesia whatsoever. Brazil is an incredible country."

The audience fell silent. They were impressed. Dr. Grof concluded his speech simply by saying: "The name of that German doctor who died eighty years ago is Dr. Fritz. Thank you for listening. *Obrigado*." As he left the stage, the hall filled with applause, but I just sat there in shock, muttering to myself, "Oh gosh, I didn't expect to hear the name of Dr. Fritz so soon!"

May 18

True to the theme of the conference, "Technology of the Sacred," methods and techniques for directly experiencing the universe and God were spotlighted over and over. Since hearing Dr. Grof's opening address, my curiosity about the rich and multi-faceted spiritual life of Brazilians was growing, so I participated in as many different workshops and sessions about these extraordinary spiritual resources as I could. I learned about a native psychedelic plant called ayahuasco, a hallucinogen legally available in Brazil. Some Christian cults, such as Branquinha and União de Vegetal, use ayahuasco in their spiritual ceremonies. Luckily, I was invited by the workshop presenter, a member of a religion called Santo Daime, to participate in one of these ceremonies that evening.

After dinner, I went down to the hotel lobby dressed in the white shirt and white pants I had been instructed to wear. When I got off the elevator, I discovered I was not alone. There were nearly 100 white-clad doctors and scholars waiting there too.

We boarded the buses that came to fetch us, and after an hour of bumpy driving, arrived at a small church surrounded by dark jungle. There we were greeted politely and briskly by high school students dressed in white uniforms, who guided us into an open-air, octagonal-shaped church. Inside, we found lots of lighted candles, a statue of the Virgin Mary, and an altar in the center laden with pictures of Santo Daime saints. After a brief ceremony, everyone—from ten-year-old girls to eighty-year-old women—drank a tea made from the ayahuasco plant. We guests were also given a half cup of the dark brown liquid, which tasted awful. Although it was bitter and smelly, I thought of it as medicine for my psyche, so I drank it all.

Then the music began. All the disciples—men and women, young and old—shook metallic *maracas* and chanted Santo Daime sacred songs. A dozen young boys sitting in a circle around the altar played guitars. The chanting went on and on, and some of the people began getting high and having ecstatic visions. Most of the guests, including me, were inexperienced with ayahuasco tea. Two hours after ingesting it, I began to feel nauseated. Clapping my hand over my mouth, I stumbled out of the church. Several of the high school students were waiting outside. They took me by the hand and led me into the jungle to the official vomiting place. Again, I was not alone. All around me, I could hear others retching. As I lost everything in my stomach, I thought, "What kind of religion is this? This is too far-out for me!" I gazed through the silhouettes of jungle trees at the night sky. The light from the billions of stars shining there was incredibly bright, and the entire sky moved like a tapestry blowing in a gentle wind. To my tripping eyes, the heavens looked like a huge Christmas decoration. Again with impeccable manners, the high school student who was watching over me led me back inside the church.

The main purpose of this ceremony and its location, I concluded, was to accumulate a magnetic field of spiritual energy. Then, with a little help from the sacred chanting and the power of the ayahuasco tea, we would attempt to create higher, more refined vibrations to aid in the ascension of our collective consciousness. Consequently, I felt obliged to cooperate with everyone, to maintain my intention and contribute toward heightening the energy field inside this psychedelic church. After a while, I looked at my watch and found that four hours had passed; it was after midnight.

Finally, the sacred chanting came to an end and someone turned on the church's electric lights. I thought, "Finally, it's over!" But I was wrong. It was only time to drink the second round of tea. The chant continued for at least two more hours before the lights came up again. Again I felt, this time with a deeper relief, "Finally, this is over!"

Wrong again. The church's priest and charismatic leader, Alex Polari de Alverga, stood before us, his long white beard brushing his chest, and declared, "Ladies and gentlemen, now our work and ceremony comes to the final stages. For the vibrations of bliss and ecstasy, let us work hard together."

All the chairs on which we were sitting were removed from the church by the high school students, and from then on all of us stood and danced and sang a sacred chant. Roughly translated from the Portuguese, the chant goes something like this: "The stars, the earth, the wind, the ocean/all the bright lights of the sky/the light I adore and love/I always remember the universal divine energy of heaven."

We took very simple steps to the right and left, dancing slowly around the circle and singing the song. To tell the truth, I really wanted to escape, to be by myself and commune with Mother Nature. But I reminded myself that we were guests, and therefore had an obligation to contribute and cooperate with the energetic ascension. Arny Mindell was dancing and singing next to me. He is the originator of process-oriented psychology. I could tell by the expression on his face that he was feeling the same reluctance.

At last, the ceremony came to an end, and we were brought back to our hotel by bus. It was five o'clock in the morning.

May 19

I was exhausted from the all-night Santo Daime ceremony, but I pushed myself to wake up and get to the morning workshop session. On the way there, I met Baba Ram Dass, my spiritual hero. He was standing by himself on the walkway reading some sort of pamphlet. I felt a very compassionate, attractive vibration emanating from him, so after a moment's hesitation, I decided to talk with him.

"Excuse me, Dr. Ram Dass. I've been a big fan of yours for many many years," I said.

He gave me a cheek-to-cheek smile. "That's great," he said. "Thank you so much." Then he put his arms around me, hugging me so tightly he nearly lifted me off the ground. I could feel his big hands at my back, pulling me into his large spongy body. I felt instantly happy, and decided to take advantage of this rare opportunity to ask him something I had been pondering for a long time.

"Dr. Ram Dass," I began, "I write a regular four-page column for a Japanese New Age magazine, but since the subway nerve gas attack by the Aum Shinrikyo cult, a lot of Japanese have a negative image of New Age and spiritual practices. Do you have any suggestions for our friends in Japan? I would really appreciate your advice."

He looked deeply into my eyes and said, "That is not an easy question to answer right away. I'd like to put this question in my heart and let it sit there for a while, so give me a little time to think about it." Then he walked away.

That afternoon, by coincidence, I met him on the walkway several times. Each time, he said, "Not yet. I don't have the answer yet." I almost gave up hope, but after dinner, at the entrance to the restaurant, he sat down with me and said, "The crime committed by the cult in Japan was a very unfortunate incident for people who meditate regularly. At some level of the journey toward awakening, it is useful to have other people share the experience with you. But ultimately, every person needs to face their God or Spirit by themselves, alone. When I was in Japan, I felt that Japanese people have a very big, very pure passion for spiritual experience. That's why Japan was so wounded by this event. But in time, the wound will certainly heal. Then, I believe the Japanese will welcome a new era of love and spirituality."

The sincerity of Ram Dass's soft-spoken words impressed me deeply. His energy was so warm and comforting that I admired him all the more.

May 20

This was the fifth day of the conference. By noon the following day, it would all be over. Before I came to Manaus, I thought that an academic conference like this might be the wrong place for a high school dropout like me. But now that the experience was almost over, I thought how lucky I was to have had a week like this, full of knowledge, stimulation, and fun.

Especially important to me was the opportunity to learn the essence of the various spiritual traditions of Brazil from the most qualified teachers of each sect. God truly is alive here in Brazil, and with many faces!

After our final dinner, I returned to my room to prepare for the next day's departure. But I couldn't find a brochure about the "Mind of the Earth" that I wanted to take home with me. The brochure described a phenomenon that was to occur on January

23, 1997. On that date, planet Earth's astrological chart would become the shape of David's six-pointed star. It was an opportunity to pray and meditate, connecting with people all around the world. When I got back to Boulder, I planned to fax this brochure to my friends on the New Age circuit in Japan, so that they could participate.

I searched my room again and again but couldn't find the brochure, so I decided to go back to the hotel lobby to get another. When I got there, however, there were no more to be found. I was a little disappointed, but before going back to my room, I located a large bulletin board nearby. Scanning the entire board, I finally found, at the very top left, the last sample of the "Mind of the Earth" brochure. As I moved closer to copy down the information I wanted, my eye was drawn to something next to the brochure. Pinned down with a thumbtack was a simple piece of paper on which someone had scribbled in Magic Marker: "Video showing of *Dr. Fritz—Healing the Spirit.*"

Suddenly, the piece of paper seemed to grow really huge. Excitedly, I looked for information about the time of the showing. It read, "Tonight at 10 p.m. in the Rio Negro Hall." I looked at my watch. It was a little past ten.

Suddenly, I didn't care anymore about the "Mind of the Earth." I ran upstairs to the hall and opened the door. Inside, it was dark and the video had already begun. When my eyes adjusted to the darkness, I realized that the hall was full, so I sat down in a metal folding chair in the very back of the room and squinted at the screen. I could just make out a vague image of a young doctor treating a patient, but because the video was projected onto a big screen, it was faded and difficult to see, especially from my vantage point. Even so, I could tell that this doctor was poking a patient's eyeballs with scissors. In another scene, he had cut open a patient's back, and the patient was talking while the operation proceeded. I could barely hear one of the male patients in the video as he held an X-ray photograph up for the camera and said, "My doctor in a big hospital gave up treating me anymore because I had an inoperable tumor. But Dr. Fritz operated on me. Now look at this X-ray. All the cancer cells have disappeared."

The more I saw, the more curious I became, and I tried to watch the screen more closely. But all of a sudden, the video stopped and a man with red eyeglasses came up on the stage. Introducing himself as the producer of the video, he said, "I've been researching and filming the Dr. Fritz phenomenon for the past five years. Right now, I'm in the middle of editing this video. I'm sorry the image wasn't very clear. I just wanted to show the first ten minutes as a sample."

Just as I was thinking, "What? Is that all?" another short film came on. Although I couldn't see this one clearly either, I felt excitement growing in my heart. Like it or not, I found myself reacting to this thing they called the "Dr. Fritz phenomenon." I tried to resist, telling myself, "Hey, Maki, don't get so excited. You have a tendency to get overenthusiastic way too easily."

Trying to calm myself, I returned to my room.

May 21

The closing ceremony of the conference ended before noon. Downstairs, the hotel lobby was jammed with people checking out. I had a little time before my flight to Rio de Janeiro, so I decided to sample the Brazilian lunch buffet. Laid out on a big table in the restaurant were many cuisines typical of Brazil, such as churrasco and feijoada, grilled meat dishes, and the deep fried Amazonian fish called pirarucu. I couldn't even tell what a lot of the dishes were. While I was busy deciding among the selections, I noticed a gentleman across the buffet table who was piling his plate high with salad. He was Caucasian and wore red eyeglasses. Suddenly I recognized him as the producer of the Dr. Fritz video I had seen the night before. Grateful for this fortuitous coincidence in the final minutes of my stay, I asked, "Would you join me at my table?" He accepted my offer, and I was glad of the chance to get a closer look at him. He had a refined intelligent air about him.

As we sat down together, he introduced himself as David Sonnenschein. "I graduated from the same California film college as George Lucas," he told me. "Ten years ago, I married a Brazilian woman, and I've been living in Rio de Janeiro ever since, making big-screen movies."

"What a coincidence!" I said. "I'm going to Rio this afternoon without hotel reservations, and I could use some advice on finding a place to stay for nine days." He gave me the names of several nice, clean, inexpensive hotels on Ipanema Beach.

Soon a lot of people came to our table to say good-bye to him, so we didn't get a chance to talk much more. However, when we finished our lunches, David gave me his home phone number and told me, "I'm going back to Rio in three or four days. Feel free to call me. If you get a chance, it might be a good idea to meet Dr. Fritz."

"The person who channels Dr. Fritz's spirit lives in Rio?"

"Oh, yes," he said, "In fact, he lives in the apartment right next door to me!" He gave me a wink, and left the table.

As I sat there alone at a table for six, I remembered the green eyes of the strange woman at the Miami airport and the words she said to me: "I'm pretty sure you are going to meet Dr. Fritz." I remembered, too, the tickling sensation on my ear as she whispered those words.

All this synchronicity meant something, I felt. I couldn't simply dismiss these coincidences as flukes. It was as though I was being manipulated by an incredibly huge energy from somewhere.

Returned from World War I

May 24

On the fourth night of my stay in Rio de Janeiro, I was able to reach David by telephone. "I'm sorry," he said. "I just got back, and I'm too busy to go with you tomorrow." But he gave me the address of Dr. Fritz's clinic.

Should I go meet this Dr. Fritz tomorrow? My inner skeptic argued, "What can you possibly hope to gain by meeting this doctor? He's probably bogus." But my curiosity won me over, and before going to sleep, I decided to seek out this miracle worker the next day.

May 25

Early the next morning, I went down to the hotel lobby and asked the desk clerk how long it would take me to get to the Penha district.

He raised his eyebrows a little and asked, "Why do you need to go to the Penha district? I don't really recommend going to an area like that." It sounded like a warning, and I began to feel a little worried.

"So the Penha district is a dangerous ghetto, like the ones I've read about in the newspapers?"

"No, no, no," he said. "It's not that bad." But I could still hear the reluctance in his voice.

Feeling pretty uneasy about my excursion, I left my camera and wallet in the hotel safe, taking just enough money to pay for a taxi. I hailed the first one that came by. The driver didn't seem to have the faintest idea of how to get there. As we drove for miles through dilapidated industrial areas, he stopped and shouted to pedestrians along the way: "Dr. Fritz? Dr. Fritz?" After an exhausting search, we finally found the Penha district and Dr. Fritz's hospital. It was just past noon. Feeling a little sorry for the driver because he had lost his voice from shouting, I gave him a good tip, and stepped out onto the sidewalk.

When I turned to look at the hospital across the street, I was very surprised. This big building, on the corner of Rua Quito and Rua Couto, looked nothing like any hospital I had ever seen. In fact, it was a dilapidated warehouse that had been abandoned many years before. The paint was peeling off the outside walls, and the windows that weren't broken were very dirty. It made me sad. How could this be the hospital that Dr. Stanislav Grof spoke so highly of?

Outside the front gates of the building, the scene reminded me of a festival at an Indian temple. Everywhere I looked there were people and vendors selling fruit juice and bread and incense to the crowd gathered there.

After taking the scene in for a few minutes, I decided to venture inside. Once through the gates, I was amazed to find even more people, packed wall to wall. Somehow I managed to make my way through them into another huge hall with a high ceiling covered in broken roof tiles. I couldn't believe my eyes! Inside this hall were another few hundred people. Most of the patients, dressed in cheap clothing, were obviously poor. Thirty or forty people sat in wheelchairs, and others leaned on crutches. Still others had bandages over their eyes.

"How the hell can Dr. Fritz treat all of these patients," I wondered with amazement. "There's no way one human being can fix all of these people. It's impossible."

I needed to calm down. To bring myself down to earth, I decided to count the number of patients. I divided the people into units of about one hundred and began to multiply. I counted once, then twice, then a third time. The number I got was about one thousand. How could one doctor single-handedly treat a thousand patients in one day? My curiosity was piqued, and I began to feel a sort of glimmering around my body.

About a dozen workers, wearing name tags, were organizing the patients. Another dozen or more nurses, in white uniforms, were busily preparing treatments. I searched their faces, but couldn't find anyone who looked like Dr. Fritz. Eventually, I saw what looked like a clinic room beyond the main room. As I started to go through the door, two young Brazilians, who had been organizing the patients, blocked the way. I explained to them in English that Dr. Fritz's neighbor, the movie director David Sonnenschein, had told me about Dr. Fritz, and assured them that it was okay for me to go inside. They didn't seem to understand me, but somehow I found myself inside the rather large clinic room. To my surprise, here were another 200 or so patients waiting very quietly in a dozen straight lines.

Beneath the windows along one side of the room sat about twenty obviously very ill patients in wheelchairs, attended by relatives who were looking after them. I could see the pain and anxiety in their faces.

Slowly, I became aware of some familiar music playing faintly in the background, though the noise from the crowd in the big hall next door made it difficult to hear. At first I thought, "It can't be," but when I put my ear up to a small speaker hanging from a wall, I could hear the strains of a Hindu *bhajan,* a prayerful song to a Hindu god. Two years before, when I was on a pilgrimage to Indian temples, I heard the same song many times. It was a song of praise to the gods Rama and Krishna. I couldn't believe I was hearing the same bhajan in a place like this. I felt something like a sacred vibration and was in awe that this vibration could reach out and make connections beyond time and space. It was deeply moving.

I looked around again and noticed a picture of the Holy Mother and other saints on the opposite wall. Beneath these sacred pictures sat a simple wooden desk and a white metal folding chair. Atop the desk stood a small statue of Jesus Christ and a vase filled with pink roses. The beauty of the flowers drew me closer, and I breathed in their fragrance. All of a sudden, I thought, "This must be Dr. Fritz's desk!"

Just then, two middle-aged nurses appeared and began speaking to me in Portuguese. I could tell they weren't trying to chase me away, because they were very polite and friendly, but they spoke very rapidly, and I couldn't understand them at all. I struggled to think how I could communicate with them. It seemed no one in the clinic spoke English. Then a powerful looking older nurse came over. She seemed to be the chief nurse, and she said to me in broken English, "Here English-speaking person. Now I bring him." Five minutes later, she came back, accompanied by a young Brazilian man wearing thick eyeglasses. He was very friendly and lively, and wore a white T-shirt and blue jeans. He smiled animatedly and asked me what country I came from and if there was anything I needed. I was very happy to find someone I could talk with.

I told him I had come to learn about Dr. Fritz, and he smiled broadly and pointed to a simple black-and-white portrait, drawn in charcoal or pencil, hanging on the wall. "This is Dr. Fritz," he said. "He was a surgeon in the German army who died in World War I. But the spirit of Dr. Fritz comes here and miraculously cures people."

I supposed this young man was a worker in this place. I liked him immediately, and decided this was a good opportunity to ask some questions. But suddenly he put his hand on my mouth and said, "I'm sorry, I have other business to attend to. Please take your time and enjoy your visit here."

As I watched him walk into the back room, I was a little disappointed that I wasn't going to learn more about Dr. Fritz, but I had that happy feeling around my chest that I get whenever I meet a wonderful person.

I stepped over to the framed portrait of Dr. Fritz hanging on the wall and examined it more closely. It was a simple copy made from an original. It depicted a fat European man with a humorous expression on a bespectacled bearded face. Written on the portrait were the words, "Dr. Adolph Fritz, died 1915." It was bizarre to think that Dr. Fritz had died more than eighty years ago, yet somehow was still alive in this hospital.

As I stood contemplating the portrait, the door to the back room opened and the same young man emerged, now dressed all in white. He walked to the little desk and slowly looked around at the people in the room, smiling as if to say good-bye. Then he sat down on the folding chair and several nurses gathered around him and closed their eyes. Then they raised their hands to about shoulder height and turned their palms outward toward the young man. It seemed as though they were sending some sort of prayer energy to him.

He took off his thick eyeglasses, gently laid them on the desk, gazed at the little statue of Jesus Christ for a few seconds, then put his right elbow on the desk. With his right hand, he covered both his eyes and became very quiet. It felt like time stood still, and I gazed at him with wonder and awe. Perhaps twenty seconds of silence had passed when his head and hand slipped from his eyes and his head dropped closer to the desk's surface. Slowly then, he raised his face, and I saw it was not the same friendly face I had seen only thirty seconds before. His entire complexion had become reddish, and his eyes, without the thick glasses now, were half open and had a sort of sleepy look. At that moment, I realized with some surprise that the friendly young man was really Dr. Fritz himself.

Though I had seen the video of Dr. Fritz at the conference in Manaus, the image had been so distorted that I hadn't recognized this young Brazilian as him. "Can this really be happening?" I wondered. "Can the spirit of a doctor who died nearly eighty years ago manifest himself again through the body of another? Perhaps this young man has some kind of psychiatric disease, like multiple personality disorder, and loses himself in playing the role of this historical personality Dr. Fritz."

My mind was too Westernized to understand or accept this phenomenon, even though it had just happened right in front of me. I noticed the impatience of my rational mind, and realized that it didn't know what to do when faced with a situation it couldn't easily understand. I decided I didn't need to come to a rational conclusion just then. The only thing I could do was closely observe this phenomenon while trying to keep a cool researcher's eye. To calm down, I inhaled deeply three times. Then I focused all my attention on Dr. Fritz again.

The chief nurse brought in about two hundred forms, which had been filled out by first-time clients, and placed them on the desk in front of Dr. Fritz. Each piece of paper described the symptoms or illness of a different patient. Dr. Fritz began sorting the papers into two stacks, one for patients requiring immediate treatment and the other for patients whom he could see later. The speed with which he sorted the forms was beyond my imagination. He spent no more than one or two seconds on each, placing it to the right or left. That could only mean he was not reading the papers, I realized, but sorting them by feel.

Sometimes he would stop and turn his head a little. Then, without looking at the page, he would place his finger on the surface and move it to the right or left. I guessed that he must be sensing how serious the patient's illness was through his fingertip. I couldn't understand how he did this. It just blew my mind.

In the middle of this work, he looked up and spoke to the chief nurse, and his voice was totally different from the voice I had heard before he channeled Dr. Fritz. The young mans' soft, rather sweet voice had become husky and low.

In fewer than ten minutes, he finished sorting the papers, arose from the table, and walked into the back room, accompanied by a few nurses. As he did so, he passed right in front of me. I tried to read his facial expression, whether he noticed me or not. There was no sign he remembered me, even though we had met only fifteen minutes before.

After they were gone, another nurse came to me and began pointing toward the room where Dr. Fritz had gone, saying, "Dr. Fritz. Operação." She repeated this until I understood that Dr. Fritz was performing an operation in the other room. Next to the door of that room, I saw a poster of a nurse with her finger to her lips. Underneath the picture was printed the word "*Silencio*," or

"Silence." I became very curious about what was going on behind that door, but it seemed to be a sacrosanct area that no one could enter without permission. So for the time being, I waited on the other side with two hundred others.

After about an hour, Dr. Fritz emerged with a more serious expression than before. Three nurses were waiting for him with a rolling cart full of hypodermic needles filled with a dark brown liquid. As soon as he came into the room, he picked up one of the needles and began injecting the patients at the front of the line.

He spoke one or two words to each patient, then injected the needle rather randomly into some part of his or her body, seemingly paying little attention to what he was doing. The speed at which he diagnosed and injected each patient was beyond my ability to comprehend. Some patients had brought an X-ray with them. Dr. Fritz would hold the X-ray up to the electric light for about five seconds, explain something to them, and then inject them very quickly. He used a new needle for each person, but it seemed as though all the fluid in the needles was the same. I wondered if the dark brown liquid was some kind of magical miracle wonder drug that was suitable for everyone.

There were many children and babies in the room, as well. I know children can be very sensitive to pain, especially injections, but not one child expressed any pain when injected. In fact, hardly any children in that room were crying. Dr. Fritz appeared very fond of them. He gave each one a big smile, sometimes pinching them affectionately or touching their head or body in a joyful friendly way.

Some patients he injected near the eyes, others near the nose, others in the back of the neck. The needles were quite long. I watched the people closely as they were injected. Most didn't change their facial expression at all. It seemed they felt no pain whatsoever. I saw one old man being injected in his spine, the long needle penetrating deeply into his body. All the while he smiled and talked with Dr. Fritz.

Dr. Fritz finished treating these two hundred or so patients in about two hours. Watching all this, I became so moved that I felt like crying. Perhaps some pure part of my mind was reacting to some kind of energy vibrations overflowing from Dr. Fritz.

All at once, I felt I understood the true meaning of my unexpected nine days in Rio de Janeiro. I had thought it was the tour company's mistake, but now I understood that the universe was offering me an opportunity to meet Dr. Fritz. I didn't know what would happen or what I would do, but I had at least five days left. "This will help my spiritual growth in some new and different way," I thought. "I must come back here as much as I can for the next five days." I stayed by Dr. Fritz's side until nine o'clock that evening, although I couldn't communicate in English with anyone.

Finally, Dr. Fritz finished treating all one thousand patients, and began injecting the remaining nurses and workers. Looking at his face, I could see that the many hours of non-stop treatment had made him very tired. His complexion reddened visibly as he went along, and became more and more severe. His voice deepened even further, and sometimes he yelled at people.

Finally, his work done, he sat down on the same white folding chair where he had started out eight hours before. The older members who remained raised their hands toward him. Then, in exactly the same manner as before, he covered his eyes with his right hand, his head dropped toward the desk, and Dr. Fritz disappeared. In a few seconds, the nice young Brazilian man was back.

It was a very dramatic transformation. His face changed completely, and he replaced his eyeglasses. Smiling softly, he looked around the room at everyone. He was young and friendly again. He stood up, walked over to me, shook my hand, and said in a cheerful voice, "So how was it? How did you like Dr. Fritz?"

"I was very moved," I said. "Is it okay for me to come back tomorrow?"

He smiled broadly and said, "Oh yes, yes please! You are very very welcome here." Then he walked out of the hospital with his wife, who had been tending to paperwork throughout the day.

When they had gone, I took a moment to reflect upon what I had seen. I felt as though I'd had several weeks' experience in one day. Even after I returned to my hotel, my mind overflowed with so many questions that I finally had to make a conscious decision to stop thinking about it and go to sleep.

HIS MIRACLE SHOT:
ALCOHOL, IODINE, AND TURPENTINE

May 26

I arrived at the clinic by taxi at eleven in the morning, having left my camera at the hotel again. I wanted to take some photographs at some point, but I had no intention of writing about my experience.

There were already nearly a thousand patients gathered in the large hall. I felt clearer today, as if I could see more. Perhaps I was more acclimated, having been there the day before. Walking down the lines from beginning to end, I saw none of the same faces I had seen yesterday. That meant nearly two thousand patients had visited the place in two days.

During a moment of boredom, I walked around the abandoned warehouse clinic and happened upon a big kitchen at the end of a hallway. There I discovered eight elderly women cooking huge amounts of vegetables. To my delight, one cheerful and enthusiastic woman spoke a little English. When I asked her what she was doing, she pointed to the large stove and said, "Can't you see the huge pot? We are cooking vegetable soup for the hundreds of people here."

"Do you sell it?" I asked.

She shook her head vigorously from side to side. "No! It's free, of course. These patients get here at seven in the morning and stand in line for many hours. Their treatment may not happen until the evening, or even midnight. They must be hungry by now." She tapped my shoulder playfully with a big smile. The first batch of soup was ready. A few workers put dozens of paper cups full of soup onto a tray and began serving the patients in the large hall.

I asked this delightful woman, "Do you have any idea how many people are working here?"

"Today, about thirty of us," she said. "Different ones come here each day. Most of us, including me, are people who were cured of incurable diseases by Dr. Fritz. That's why we want to help others. Most of us are volunteers. I'm not getting any money from this work."

Now I finally felt as though I could understand the warm and caring ambiance that filled this clinic. The high quality of the energy was not coming from Dr. Fritz alone. The unconditional love of the volunteers who were awakened and inspired by Dr. Fritz was also contributing to the positive energy. All of the workers seemed very cheerful and enthusiastic, and were kind to those around them. It seemed as though they were expressing their feelings with actions, rather than words. I imagined how they must feel—very happy simply to be alive and healthy.

Before I left the kitchen, I asked the woman for the name of the young man who channels Dr. Fritz, something I still hadn't learned. "His name is Rubens Faria," she said. "He used to be a computer engineer who graduated from the IME, the Institute of Military Engineering. He looks like a young man, but I hear he's forty-two years old. Rubens is a wonderful person." I thought, "What? This young man is from the same generation as me?"

At about one o'clock in the afternoon, when everyone had finished eating their soup, a young black nurse began to lead a prayer in the large hall. A few people ignored the prayer, but most closed their eyes and repeated the sacred words. Some raised both hands towards the sky and appeared deeply absorbed. Others joined their palms together in front of their chest. Some had tears on their cheeks.

At first, watching this scene reminded me of the proverb "A drowning man will grasp at a straw," but when I considered the deeper meaning of these prayers, I concluded that pain can enable people to connect with a higher level of being and thus have the opportunity to be reborn to a new level of consciousness. As I looked around at the volunteers, working so hard and selflessly, and at the patients, praying so deeply from the heart, I thought, "Maybe more genuinely spiritual things are happening right now in this dilapidated warehouse than at any elaborate church or gorgeous famous temple."

Just then, without any announcement or fanfare, Rubens and his wife walked rapidly into the room. As they came in, the people in the large hall began spontaneously applauding. Rubens looked rather shy, but he smiled and raised his hand in greeting. The couple passed quickly through the large hall and into the clinic room. Being the earnest spiritual-supermarket shopper that I am, I've seen many famous gurus and enlightened people—the Dalai Lama, Osho Rajneesh, Sai Baba, Chogyam Trungpa Rinpoche, to name a few—enter a room where people were awaiting them. But nearly every supposedly enlightened guru did so with some religious, contrived, and even stagy ceremony. Although I have no intention of including Dr. Fritz in the category of guru or religious leader, I can't help but find the naturalness of his entry refreshing.

Following him into the clinic room, I arrived just as he was about to sit down on the folding chair. He turned, recognized me, and gave me a friendly handshake. "Thank you so much for coming again," he said. "I have something interesting to show you." As he spoke, he took off his eyeglasses and handed them to me. I looked through the lenses and everything appeared blurry because they were so thick. "As you see," he said, "I am absolutely myopic, with an astigmatism. Without these eyeglasses, I am like a blind person. I can't see anything. But when I incorporate Dr. Fritz's spirit into myself, he can see everything without glasses, inside and out. The explanation is: I can't explain it. He knows why. I don't know anything about it."

I wanted to ask him a lot of questions about his career as a computer engineer and how he began channeling Dr. Fritz, but Rubens had already put on his white coat and was ready to begin. Speaking with him for ten minutes is equivalent to the time he takes to treat at least twenty people, so I decided not to ask too many questions.

Rubens sat down in the chair exactly as he had the day before, smiled at everyone, removed the eyeglasses, and covered both eyes with his right hand. Again there were the few sacred seconds, and I began to hear energy flowing inside my eardrums. It sounded like a hummingbird, a gentle, soothing thrumming. As I listened to this inner sound, I thought, "It's coming again." Ever since I began practicing meditation many years ago, whenever I meet a wonderful guru or admire beautiful flowers or after great blissful sex, I hear this sound. I assume it's the sound of my inner energy flowing, so I wasn't surprised to hear it again as Rubens channeled Dr. Fritz. It simply reconfirmed Dr. Fritz's level of energy. To me, that sound is a manifestation of a profound deeper experience within.

Suddenly Rubens dropped his head towards the desk and became Dr. Fritz. Just as before, he sorted out new patients' forms with superhuman speed. Then he went into the operating room. I had learned that he operates on about twenty people a day, in addition to treating some one thousand others with injections. I wished that I could watch him operate. I had heard he operated without anesthesia, and I hoped to witness this before I left Rio.

While Dr. Fritz was in the operating room, I took a walk through the large hall, where I came across clinic workers collecting the treatment fees. I had been wondering how they managed to run such a huge clinic, even though most of the staff seemed to be volunteers. I watched with interest as two older nurses walked between the lines of patients collecting money in something similar to a church donation box. As far as I could tell, most people put in a $10 bill, but it seemed like the poorer-looking people didn't have to put money in. They previous day, I thought I had seen some patients being given medication for free, and I heard they were not being charged for operations. I worried a little about the financial management, because Rubens doesn't have a medical license, which means that his treatments can't be covered by medical insurance.

As I pondered this, I noticed the cheerful woman from the kitchen waving at me to get my attention. I followed her toward what appeared to be a storage room. It was kind of dark, so it took a moment for my eyes to adjust. Then I saw big piles of food and clothing. The woman explained: "People who were cured by Dr. Fritz, they come back day after day to donate these things. We deliver them to the poor, to nearly 500 people a month."

I thanked her for the information and headed back to the clinic room, where Dr. Fritz was already at work treating the more severely ill, wheelchair-bound patients. There were all sorts of miserable people there, kids with misshapen legs, an old man with elephantiasis whose leg looked like a fat tire, a middle-aged woman who had a festering sore on her breasts, perhaps terminal breast cancer. The symptoms of some patients were so gross that I felt like turning my face away. I had to tell myself many times to face reality and keep observing. I must admit, I am one of those people who can't stand hospitals.

I tried to move closer to Dr. Fritz. He was talking to a very respectable-looking older man in a wheelchair, behind whom a young clever-looking man stood, perhaps his son. Dr. Fritz was using a longer needle than usual to inject the patient, and he sank it twice deeply into the man's spine. From the quality of the clothing the two were wearing, I thought that perhaps one of them might speak English. When they left the room, I chased after them and asked if that was so. The old man said, "Not well, but I do speak some." His voice was rather weak. Because of the language barrier, I hadn't had much of a chance to talk with any patients. I decided to step into journalist mode and interview these two.

"I'm an attorney in Rio de Janeiro," the older man told me. "If you're a Brazilian journalist, I really don't want to talk with you."

"Oh, don't worry," I replied. "I'm Japanese. I'm not going to publish anything in Brazil." Then I asked, "How many times have you come here to the clinic?"

"Today is the first time," he said. "I have had cancer in my vertebrae for six months. I've gone to nearly all the big famous hospitals in Rio, but all the doctors told me that even with all the most modern Western medical techniques, they couldn't do anything for me; it was just too late. Nowadays, I can't sleep at all, even with morphine injections three times a day. A friend of mine recommended Dr. Fritz. That's why I came today."

"What did you talk with Dr. Fritz about?" I asked.

"I briefly described my symptoms. Dr. Fritz told me that today, somehow, he can stop the pain, but he asked me to bring the X-rays back in three days. Then he will decide whether to operate or not."

Somehow, I was a little disappointed. I had finally found someone I could interview, but he was not an example of anything like an instant cure. However, he said he would be coming back in three days, on my last day in Rio, so I said, "Thank you very much. I'll be here in three days, too, so I'll see you again. Goodbye."

Back in the large hall, about two hundred patients were waiting for treatment and gradually moving toward the preparatory clinic room under the direction of the workers. It seemed as though keeping people quiet was the main goal. It was natural for so many people to want to talk and chat, which created a lot of noise. Every time it got loud, the workers would put their fingers in front of their lips and say, "Shhhh."

After treating the two hundred or so patients inside the clinic room, Dr. Fritz moved into the preparatory room, where he treated another two hundred. Then he would go back to the operating room, perform surgery on seven or eight patients, and then begin all over again, injecting another two hundred patients. This seemed to be his system. He treated patients for about ten hours without taking a break. Once in a while, he would drink some juice brought to him by a nurse. Then, at night, when his body became really tired, he injected the same brown liquid into the back of his own neck. That seemed to give him the energy he needed to go on.

I was very curious about the contents of the hypodermic needles. After seven at night, I sneaked away from the clinic to get something to eat. Nearly three hundred patients were still waiting inside. As I bit into a boiled, salted ear of corn that I had bought from one of the street vendors out front, I heard a voice behind me ask in perfect American English, "Are you from Japan?" I turned and saw a short, plump, elderly gentleman standing there. He shook my hand very firmly and introduced himself as Eduardo. "I was born here in Brazil," he told me, "but emigrated to the United States when I was twenty. Now I own several restaurants in upstate New York. Nice to meet you here."

I was happy to finally meet someone who could speak English fluently. "What a coincidence," I said. "My name is Maki. I went to the United States seventeen years ago, and now I own a rock 'n' roll sushi bar in Boulder, Colorado."

He proceeded to tell me about his experience with Dr. Fritz, and it just blew my mind, shaking up my common sense and threatening all my stereotypes. Here is his story: Eduardo's business in New York expanded year by year, bringing with it a lot of stress and frustration. He became ill with stomach and bone marrow cancer simultaneously. The New York doctors gave up on him, and he decided, "If I'm going to die, I would like it to be in my mother's country." So he returned to Brazil a year ago. Then he heard a rumor about Dr. Fritz. He didn't believe it but thought he would give the man a try anyway. "Over two months, Dr. Fritz operated on me four times," he said. "I regained a lot of energy, and when I returned to New York, I had an extensive check-up in the hospital. They found that both the stomach and bone marrow cancers were completely healed. Of course, my primary care physician was really surprised. He couldn't believe it."

I asked, "Is it true that Dr. Fritz doesn't use any anesthesia when he operates?"

"That's right," Eduardo said. "During my first operation, Dr. Fritz began cutting into my body without any warning, but miraculously, I didn't feel any pain at all. In fact, during the operation, Dr. Fritz and I cracked jokes and laughed a lot." He pulled up the front of his shirt and proudly showed me some of the scars from the operation. The two of us quickly became friends and walked back inside together.

Dr. Fritz had just finished all the operations for the day and was about to see the last two hundred patients. I looked at my watch. It was after eight, and I saw intense fatigue on his face. His voice was hoarse. Looking at his intensity, I suddenly superimposed the image of a Boddhisattva over him. The Boddhisattva are the beings in Buddhist mythology who give up their karmic reward of transcending rebirth in order to remain on the material plane and save the rest of us. I was very moved by Dr. Fritz's passionate, selfless acts.

Then I remembered something I had been wanting to ask for two days. I whispered to Eduardo, "You must know what the dark brown liquid inside the hypodermic needles is, eh?" But he only replied, "Dr. Fritz is very sensitive about chatting and noise." Taking my hand, he led me outside the room and then told me, "I heard that an American scientist was very curious about that brown liquid, so he brought it to a NASA laboratory for testing. They discovered it was made up of alcohol, iodine, and turpentine."

"What?!" I said loudly. "Turpentine?!" Many years before, I had had a house-painting business in Berkeley, California, and I used turpentine as a solvent for oil-based paints. To me, turpentine is just a powerful-smelling paint thinner. It would be out of the question to even put it into your mouth. If you were to inject it into your body, you would be committing suicide.

Eduardo calmly told me, "Yes, it is turpentine. Of course, if a regular doctor used this, it would be deadly. But you must understand that Dr. Fritz is connected to a higher vibration in the universe, beyond the reach of normal people. Obviously, he uses highly evolved technology. Dr. Fritz told me that when this mixture is injected into the human body, it searches through the body's 60 trillion cells, finds the molecules of diseased cells, and breaks them up into elementary particles. Then he can reconstruct those elementary particles into healthier molecules to form healthier cells. Then healing takes place. That's how he explained it."

I tried to recall what I had learned in school. I remembered that material is made up of molecules and that molecules are made up of atoms. Atoms are made up of electrons circling at super speeds around a nucleus. The nucleus itself is made up of protons and neutrons. At even more basic levels, everything is made up of vibrations. Whew! I was becoming more confused, and honestly couldn't understand anything at all. So I gave up and asked Eduardo what I had wanted to ask before: "I've observed that they reuse the same syringes over and over all day long without sterilizing them. They just keep refilling them with that brown liquid. I'm worried about the possibility of infections being spread with contaminated needles. What do you think?"

"Nowadays, at the frontiers of Western medicine, besides disinfectants and germicides, they use ultraviolet rays to sterilize surgical equipment. Maybe it would be easier for you to understand by thinking that Dr. Fritz is using an even higher ray than ultraviolet, one that is even better at sterilizing than ultraviolet. The fact is, 350,000 patients have received medical treatment from Dr. Fritz. So far, there hasn't been one reported case of infection."

As I sat listening to his explanation, I became tired. My rational mind simply would not digest this information. It was too far beyond common sense. "All right," I said, "But why don't people feel pain when he is operating without anesthesia?"

"I don't understand this clearly either," he replied, "but I heard that Dr. Fritz can manipulate the brain waves of the patients and guide electromagnetic waves inside the patient's body. Also, this Dr. Fritz phenomenon isn't happening because of just one spirit. Besides his spirit, there are about three thousand other spirits of doctors and nurses present, and they are all helping each other. That means that the spirit of other doctors are diagnosing the patients before they come to Dr. Fritz for treatment. That doctor tells Dr. Fritz which part of the body is sick and what amount of liquid needs to be injected into what part. That's why Dr. Fritz is able to treat a thousand patients a day so efficiently."

My brain was overflowing with too much information, so I said, "Thank you very much. I think this is enough for tonight!" and returned to the clinic.

Only a few patients were still waiting for treatment, in addition to some workers and nurses who wanted treatments as well. Maybe because Dr. Fritz could see the end of the line, he was relaxed and smiling again, and talking frankly with the workers as he finished up for the night. All of a sudden, Eduardo said, "Dr.

Fritz, why don't you give this Japanese guy an injection?" Dr. Fritz looked at me with his half-opened, sleepy-looking eyes and said, "Well, I see you have one place you want to get healed."

I was very surprised by this turn of events—a little panicked, in fact. I protested, "Oh no, Dr. Fritz, I'm just an observer here. Please. No thank you." Dr. Fritz watched my comical reaction, smiled, and said, "Oh well, when you're ready, just tell me. Anytime."

I think of myself as a very healthy person. I had even run 6.2 miles that morning on Ipanema Beach. But for no apparent reason, six months before, my left shoulder had become very painful. I couldn't move it at all without pain. I had tried many different medical treatments, including alternative methods such as acupuncture and chiropractic, but nothing had cured it. I knew from reading the newspaper that there were about a half million carriers of the HIV virus in Brazil. Picturing the unsterilized hypodermic needles filled with a liquid that contained turpentine, I just didn't have the guts to get injected with such a dangerous combination.

No Anesthesia,
No Pain, No Blood

May 29

This was the last of five consecutive days at Dr. Fritz's clinic. In the last two days I had watched closely as Rubens transformed into Dr. Fritz and then back again to Rubens.

The night before, after Rubens transformed back from Dr. Fritz, Rubens told me, "No foreign visitors matching your eagerness have come here for many days. Usually foreigners come here out of curiosity, are impressed, take a few pictures, and leave three hours later. You are the first to stay for so long."

I thought this was a good opportunity to ask him a question, so I said, "For four days, there is something I have very much wanted to do—to take a picture of you operating. Is it possible for me to bring my camera and get inside the operating room to take a photo tomorrow?" He smiled, put his hand on my left shoulder, and said, "Oh yes, yes. It's no problem. A TV station is coming here tomorrow to shoot a documentary, so it might be a good chance for you to take your photographs, too."

So I had brought my favorite Contax portable camera and eight rolls of film. As I was taking photographs inside the main clinic room, I saw the old lawyer I had spoken with three days before. The last time I saw him and his son, the lawyer was in a wheelchair, but today he was sitting on a regular folding chair like the others. I remembered how pale and pained he had looked three days previous, but today he seemed more lively and at peace

~

"Hi. It's good to see you again," I said. Then I brought the camera up to my eye to take a photo of him, but he immediately blocked the lens with his hand. "Because of my highly respected occupation," he said," I don't want anyone to know that I'm here in a psychic surgeon's clinic. I'll give you an interview, but please don't use my photograph or my name in any magazine article."

I regretted my thoughtlessness and apologized. Then I said, "Your complexion looks pretty good today. How do you feel?" In a calm voice, he replied, "As I told you last time, before I came here, even though I was taking morphine shots three times a day, my spine was so painful I couldn't sleep. But since Dr. Fritz gave me this shot of brown liquid, somehow the pain is gone. So yesterday I stopped taking morphine."

Just then, Dr. Fritz walked into the main clinic room, having finished his treatments in the smaller room. Instantly, the two hundred or so patients gathered there became quiet. I ended my conversation with the lawyer, went to Dr. Fritz's side, and began taking photos of his treatments. After about thirty minutes, it was the lawyer's turn. He handed several X-rays to Dr. Fritz, who held them up to the fluorescent lights in the ceiling. As he closely examined the X-rays, he said a few words in Portuguese, and the lawyer nodded a few times. Then Dr. Fritz took an extra-long needle and pushed it deeply into the lawyer's vertebrae in two different places.

Afterwards, the lawyer and his son left, so I chased after them. When I caught up to them on the walkway, I asked, "Do you mind telling me what Dr. Fritz said to you?" This time, the son answered. "Dr. Fritz told us that if my father has surgery next week, there is ample hope of a complete recovery. But this is a very important decision, so tonight our family is going to talk it over and think about it some more."

Although it was none of my business, I said to them, "In my five days here, I have heard many stories about Dr. Fritz's abilities. If Dr. Fritz doesn't think he can cure something, he tells the patient directly. So if he says there is hope, then I would think, 'Why not give it a try?'" I bade them good-bye and went back inside.

Shortly after three, a crew of about ten people from Teve TV Globo, the local television station, rushed noisily into the main clinic room. They set up a portable lighting system, and the usually dim room was suddenly flooded with light. A good-looking middle-aged announcer with a neatly trimmed beard came into the room, accompanied by three medical doctors, and proceeded to meet with the clinic staff. I learned that his name was Domingos, and that he was something of a local celebrity. More than a few of the patients in the room asked him for his autograph.

After all the arrangements had been made, the filming began. While Dr. Fritz went about his routine injecting patients, Domingos asked him questions, thrusting his microphone in front of the doctor's face to record the reply. I guessed that he asked about the brown fluid Dr. Fritz was injecting, because Dr. Fritz walked toward the medicine counter and brought out a big white bowl. Then he held up for the camera, one at a time, bottles with labels that read "alcohol," "iodine," and "turpentine," and proceeded to mix them together in the bowl. He dipped the needle into the fluid and filled the syringe with the mixture, and then he walked over to one of the guest doctors standing nearby and injected the fluid into his neck. Domingos then interviewed the visiting doctor, and I guessed from his facial expression that he was saying he experienced no pain during the injection.

Then a young man in a wheelchair was brought into their midst. Immediately, the lights were trained on the young man, and Domingos began interviewing him. I was very curious, so I whispered to one of the guest medical doctors who spoke English, "Do you know what's wrong with him?" The doctor leaned close to my ear and explained that the young man had been involved in a shooting. One of the bullets had hit his neck and was lodged in a very critical spot near many nerves. Because of the danger of paralysis, the hospital surgeon didn't want to operate.

As I looked more closely, I noticed that the right side of the young man's neck was swollen and dark red. When the interview was over, several attendants picked up his wheelchair and carried him into the adjoining operating room. Having finally been granted entrance by

Rubens the night before, I grabbed my camera and stole quietly into the room that I had most wanted to enter for the last five days.

It was smaller than I expected, long and narrow with white walls. Six simple metal beds lay very close to one another, and on each bed lay a seriously ill patient. I noticed an annoying noise and discovered that it was coming from an antiquated air conditioner on the wall. I felt sad that inside this huge hot clinic where a thousand patients came every day, there was only one noisy old cooling apparatus. This was the reality here.

Dr. Fritz began his surgery on the young man, who remained seated in his wheelchair. I had heard about this many times, but now I saw that Dr. Fritz used no anesthesia before operating. In his left hand, he held a scalpel, and in his right hand, the handle of a stainless-steel knife, with which he began tapping on the scalpel, opening a two-inch incision on the patient's neck. It reminded me of a sculptor chiseling a wooden statue of the Buddha. Although the skin and flesh were clearly laid open, hardly any blood issued from the open wound. The tiny bit of blood that appeared around the incision was occasionally wiped off by the assisting nurse with a small piece of cotton gauze.

Dr. Fritz picked up a longer scalpel, stuck it deeply into the young man's neck, and moved it up and down. While this operation was going on, Domingos continued interviewing the young patient. I couldn't detect any expression of pain on the patient's face. Dr. Fritz even cracked some jokes, and everyone laughed. As the operation progressed, Dr. Fritz laid down the scalpel and picked up a pair of tweezers. Pushing the tweezers deeply into the young man's neck, he finally extracted a dark black bullet about 1/2 inch long. It shone with blood in the spotlight. The film crew burst into cheers.

If I were to say that this surgery was beyond the bounds of human knowledge and proved to me the existence of God, it would be an exaggeration. But I certainly felt I had to acknowledge the existence of some higher energy.

By the time the nurses began stitching up the young man's neck, the next surgery had already begun. This patient was a middle-aged man with a herniated disk. Again using the scalpel and the handle of the stainless steel knife, Dr. Fritz made an incision about three inches in length along the man's vertebrae. Again, there was no use of anesthesia of any kind. This time I tried to focus more directly on the incision, as I felt it was my duty to not look away and to observe in as much detail as possible. With my poor medical knowledge, I remembered that the area around the disks in the lower back is where the most delicate and sensitive nerves in the human body are concentrated. As Dr. Fritz began the incision, I could see fatty tissue and red muscle underneath the dermis. Although the incision looked terribly painful, again, the patient's face showed no sign of discomfort.

Then something quite unexpected happened. One of the guest medical doctors said he wanted to help, to make the incision himself. This worried me. I thought that it was only because Dr. Fritz was employing some sort of spiritual energy that no anesthesia was necessary, patients felt no pain, and only a little blood was lost. If some other doctor tried to do the same thing, what would happen? The people standing around looked a little panicked by the doctor's outrageous request, but Dr. Fritz simply smiled, nodded, and then grabbed the doctor's right arm. Closing his eyes, Dr. Fritz became quiet. It looked as though he was transferring his energy through his hand to the doctor's arm. About a minute of silence passed as the film crew looked on breathlessly. Then Dr. Fritz very slowly removed his hand from the doctor's arm and nodded, as if to say, "You are ready now." Then the medical doctor proceeded just as Dr. Fritz had, cutting the patient's skin by tapping the scalpel with the handle of the stainless-steel knife.

I was flabbergasted. People who saw this scene on television would probably think it was faked. But having observed it with my own eyes, I sensed something special about this scene. I had the impression that Dr. Fritz was creating a profoundly high energy field. It was a different kind of sensation from the one I had felt at other power centers and holy places. Here, the human body had actually been cut open without the benefit of anesthesia in front of my very eyes.

An hour later, the television crew left, looking satisfied. More than 400 people were still patiently awaiting their turn at the clinic. The film crew had finished its work, but Dr. Fritz still had much to do. I suddenly felt very sorry for Rubens for being conscripted for this job. This was really hard work. In fact, in my whole life I had never seen anyone work this hard. If it was karma, then what kind of past life had Rubens led? What kind of virtues or mistakes had he accumulated, and what kind of life would his next one be? There were no answers to my questions.

In the room next door, I found twenty patients, some with a bandage over one eye. I asked one young nurse about them, and she told me that everyone there had cataracts and had come for an operation. I had heard that the operation for cataracts is demanding, requiring focused attention, and as Dr. Fritz entered the room, I wondered how long he would spend with each of these patients. I glanced at my watch.

I looked on in disbelief as Dr. Fritz hopped from one patient to the next with incredible speed. With a scalpel in his right hand, he operated on only one eye of each patient, after which the patient received a bandage over that eye and simply walked home. Dr. Fritz used the same scalpel for all twenty surgeries. Perhaps the scalpel was sterilized by an angel or disinfected by God, and that explained why no infections were reported from this hospital. When Dr. Fritz was done, I looked again at my wristwatch and was surprised to see that it had taken a little less than twenty minutes to perform all the operations. If there were special categories in the *Guinness Book of World Records* for speed of cataract operations, then, without a doubt, Dr. Fritz would be the champion.

After he finished with the last person in the room, only the nurses and I remained. Dr. Fritz walked up to me and asked in a husky voice, "Are you sure you don't need some treatment here?" For five days, I had hesitated to ask Dr. Fritz to treat the pain in my left shoulder. At first, I was afraid of being infected by the HIV virus and of the turpentine in the brown liquid, which I knew to be deadly. However, I had observed nearly five thousand patients and more than a few healing phenomena. I began to think maybe it was about time to trust this Dr. Fritz guy. If I was going to give my body over as an experiment, today was my last chance. Suddenly I felt as though a voice within me said, "Oh well, there are risks in everything you do in life, so why not bet on the power of divine injections?" Without my conscious mind making a clear decision, my mouth opened and I heard myself say, "Okay, please do it to me."

Now I couldn't back out. A little shyly, I told him I was feeling severe pain in my left shoulder, that I couldn't even lift up my arm. Dr. Fritz said, "Oh, that's easy. No problem." Quickly, then, he thrust the hypodermic into my left shoulder. There was no sensation of pain at all, but I could feel the liquid going into my shoulder. I felt kind of happy that I had finally conquered my fear and doubt, so I said, "*Obrigado*, Dr. Fritz." Then I tried to swing my left arm in a circle and suddenly winced from the sharpness of the pain, crying out "Ouch!" I was ashamed of myself for being such a scatterbrain. Even though Dr. Fritz was a miracle healer, there was no way that the pain could disappear five seconds after the injection. Dr. Fritz smiled broadly at my silly behavior, then walked toward the main clinic room accompanied by the nurses to treat the remaining patients there. It was about seven in the evening.

Hearing a lot of English being spoken in the large hall, I went to see what was happening. There I saw about forty Americans and Europeans strolling around and realized that most of the faces were somehow familiar. Suddenly I recognized them from the conference in Manaus. As I walked over to greet them, a blond gentleman with a beard said, "Good evening. I didn't expect to see you here." It was Dr. Stephen Larsen, a psychologist and founder of the Symbolic Studies Center in New Paltz, New York. He is also the author of several books, including *The Mythic Imagination*, and *A Fire in the Mind: The Life of Joseph Campbell*, and *Shaman's Doorway*. During the ceremony at the Santo Daime Church, he had been sitting right next to me. He told me he had been leading a post-conference "Wisdom of the Serpent" tour for the past nine days. This was an unscheduled stop, but they had come because people in the group requested it.

A week before coming to Brazil, I had faxed him to ask if I

could be included on this very tour. He had told me then that the tour was full and apologized for not being able to accommodate me. Now I realized that it was only because I hadn't been able to join this tour that I had had enough time to be with Dr. Fritz for five days. It was a strange coincidence, I thought, that on the very last night of my visit, I should see these people again. Dr. Larsen related many interesting stories about their tour, and then asked, "By the way, do you know the movie director David Sonnenschein, who lives here in Rio de Janeiro?"

"Oh yes, of course," I said. "It was because of David that I was able to meet Dr. Fritz!" Then Dr. Larsen said, "Oh, that's perfect. I have a dinner date with David tonight. If you like, you can join us." Inside I jumped with joy at the chance to meet David one more time before returning to the States.

After our conversation, the tour group strolled around to observe Dr. Fritz's treatments, and then the bus came for them. I really wanted to wait for Dr. Fritz to finish all the treatments so that I could say good-bye to Rubens before leaving, but it was close to nine, and more than 100 patients were still waiting, so I decided I could only say good-bye to Dr. Fritz. I went back to the clinic room, where he was still treating patients. He looked pretty tired, but he was pushing himself to the end. Feeling a little nervous, I said, "Dr. Fritz, thank you so much for everything. Because of you I have learned immeasurable things. I am going back to the United States tomorrow."

He turned and took my hand and said, "There is some deeper meaning to your visit here. Maybe it would be a good idea to contemplate this. Thank you very much. Someday I will see you again." As he did so, I felt a soothing sensation, like a weak magnetic wave, coming through his right hand to mine.

I walked slowly out of the clinic room to the gate, where earlier in the day I had seen so many people. As I was thinking back over my five days there, it seemed as though I had been commuting to the school of Dr. Fritz for a full semester. I had two conflicting thoughts: that I had accomplished something, and that something had just begun.

The restaurant where I was supposed to meet Dr. Larsen and David was at Copacabana Beach. I was late for our appointment, and when I arrived, Dr. Larsen, his wife, and David were already drinking wine and eating. The restaurant was famous for its Bahaia cuisine, which I had heard is typical of the local cooking around the Salvador area in Brazil. Made with lots of spices and coconut milk, it looked quite exotic and was a treat for my starving stomach. By the second bottle of wine, we were waxing eloquent and getting into all sorts of cosmic topics.

After the meal, as we drank our very thick Brazilian coffee, Dr. Larsen suddenly became serious and began speaking about the Dr. Fritz phenomenon. "I am a modern man of the twentieth century," he said, "and I am skeptical about psychic surgery, despite having seen some very convincing videos and having talked to several people about it. But being in his presence is amazing. It is a feeling rather than a seeing, but the seeing and feeling go together. I'm persuaded that something absolutely real is going on, and that what we take for ordinary existence is an illusion."

My hotel was on the way to David's house, so he gave me a ride. When we got in the car, I thanked him for giving me the opportunity to meet Dr. Fritz. He asked me if I had heard the story about Dr. Fritz operating on Christopher Reeve/Superman. All of a sudden, I remembered the strange lady at the Miami airport, and I said, "Why yes! So the rumor I heard was true?" He said, "We actually don't welcome that kind of tabloid sensationalism and gossipy curiosity. Because Rubens doesn't have a medical license, it is illegal for him to treat people in the United States. A few days ago, we were offered $3,000 from the Japanese photo magazine *Friday* to give them exclusive rights to Dr. Fritz's surgery on Christopher Reeve. But we turned it down because of the sensationalism."

I asked David, "Would you mind telling me more about this? I am very interested in this story."

"Just a moment," he said, and pulled into a roadside parking area where we could talk without driving. Then he continued. "Of course, you know that he had a horseback-riding accident and seriously injured his spinal cord. He nearly died right after the accident, but he was saved with the latest cutting-edge technology that modern medical science has to offer. Now, instead of the broken spinal cord, he has a titanium pin in the shape of a croquet wicket implanted in his spine. Somehow, Christopher Reeve heard a rumor about Dr. Fritz and asked someone to investigate the possibility of getting an operation from him. When I talked with Rubens a few days ago, he told me that Dr. Fritz said, 'In this case, Mr. Reeve injured the spinal nerve very badly, so it is impossible for a complete cure. But I can make him well enough to be able to walk with a crutch.' However, Dr. Fritz said he would need to take out the titanium and rejuvenate the bone in the spinal cord."

"In English, 'rejuvenation' means becoming young again. But what does Dr. Fritz mean by the word?"

"In this case, rejuvenation can be interpreted to mean the regeneration of bone and other organs. Dr. Fritz has used this rejuvenation process on other surgery patients. He seems to have the ability to break up the cell molecules where they are bad and reunite them as healthy molecules. Unless you have ample knowledge of quantum physics, it is kind of difficult to understand, but the nucleus of a molecule is a vibration of energy, and time is also a form of energy. Somehow, Dr. Fritz is able to manipulate time energy, enabling the energy vibrations of a broken nucleus to remember the energy vibration of the healthier time in the past, thereby promoting the regeneration of healthy cells. That's how Dr. Fritz explained it. In order to rejuvenate bone, he needs to perform several surgeries on the neck and must have a period of several weeks of intense healing in between. Rubens told me he was going to New York to perform the first surgery on Reeve. That's what I heard."

I was thrilled to hear this incredible story about Dr. Fritz at midnight of my last night in Brazil. When I got out of David's car at the hotel, I gave him a present, my solo CD *Childhood Dream*, which had just been released in the American market two months before. That night, I couldn't sleep at all. I was too excited from all the intense experiences of the day.

May 30

In the morning, just before checking out of the hotel, I got a call from David. "Thank you for your CD," he said. "There are a lot of wonderful tunes on it. I really liked it, especially the second one, "Childhood Dream." It was very poetic and I was very moved. I'm editing the documentary on Dr. Fritz right now, and I would really like to use this tune as background music. May I have your permission?" I told him it would be my pleasure.

"Thank you, that's very kind of you," he said. "When I finish the video, I'll send a copy to your home in Colorado. Have a nice trip back home."

On the way to the airport, I carried a heavy bag in each hand, and I noticed that my left shoulder was not aching as it had before. I thought, "What's happened? Has Dr. Fritz's injection begun to work?" I tried moving my left arm around, slowly and gingerly. I still felt a little pain, but not the heavy ache I had felt for nearly half a year. I started to feel happy, so I moved both hands up toward the sky, as one does when one says "Banzai!" in Japan. My arm went up much higher than before, and I felt almost no pain. I muttered to myself, "Maybe it's safe to say that my experiment on my body was a success."

Later, when I calmed down, I reconsidered. In my subconscious mind, I was eager to believe the injection had a beneficial effect on me. I really wanted it to cure my left shoulder. Perhaps I was having an illusion that it worked. When a doctor gives a patient a capsule of sugar and says in a confident manner, "This is a wonder drug to cure your symptoms," the patient is often healed. This is called the "placebo effect." I didn't mind this placebo effect—but I hoped to recover completely so I could play golf again.

THE LAST VISITATION

September 18

It had been three months since I returned home from Brazil. Not even a month after my return, the ache in my shoulder was completely gone. Whether because of Dr. Fritz's shot or the effects of therapeutic exercises, the shoulder never ached anymore, even if I swam or played golf.

Unfortunately, during my trip back to Boulder from Brazil, my address book with all my telephone numbers and addresses disappeared, so I had not been able to get in contact with Rubens or David since June.

I had been working very hard putting the final touches on my debut book, *The Spiritual Adventures of a Sushi Chef,* translating it into English so it could be published by Cadence Books in San Francisco, and I was preparing to go to Japan for two months in order to complete several business projects.

That afternoon, as I was packing my suitcase, the doorbell rang. It was the postman delivering a package. When I opened it and discovered the Dr. Fritz video inside, I wanted to kiss the postman. The timing was perfect. In a flash, I closed all the blinds, pulled my chair in front of the TV, and turned on the VCR.

This ninety-minute video could be very persuasive to people skeptical about psychic surgery, perhaps as people of the sixteenth century were skeptical of Copernicus's theory. I was fascinated afresh by every scene, even though I thought I already knew a lot about the Dr. Fritz phenomenon. Viewing the first ten minutes of the video's shocking operating room scenes, sensitive people might pass out. It is not easy to watch Dr. Fritz perform brain surgery, remove a malignant tumor, or stick scissors in between people's eyelids and eyeballs. As the video progressed, Dr. Fritz explained the graphic nature of such scenes. "First, you have to shock people," he said. "When you shock them, then their consciousness can be transformed."

A renowned psychologist, Dr. Stanley Krippner of the Saybrook Institute, appears in the video. He is an outspoken advocate of the Dr. Fritz phenomenon in his books *Healing States* and *The Realm of Healing*. "I think that he's putting on a show that brings out the best in these people," Dr. Krippner says. "Technically, of course, he could do all this without cutting into the skin, without taking on the identity of Dr. Fritz. But that's not the way people's belief systems operate. People like theater, they like spectacle, they like drama, especially people who go to folk healers. Many folk healers around the world tell me, 'I would not have to call on the spirits. I would not have to cut into the body. I would not have to do the rituals, but people expect it, and I must give them what they expect if they are going to be healed.'"

In the video, several patients testify about their experience, showing X-ray photos taken before and after Dr. Fritz's treatment. One woman says, "I have femoral arthritis from an accident sixteen years ago. Because of the pain, I went to Dr. Fritz. He operated, and it's now totally improved."

A woman who is having brain surgery speaks during her operation: "I don't feel any pain." Afterwards, she says, "Dr. Fritz operated on six brain tumors in December and January. First he removed one, then the other five. I've had horrible headaches since childhood. After the first surgery, I had an eighty percent improvement. Now I have no more headaches. And the tumors were shown to be malignant."

An old man standing in front of the clinic says, "I had a clogged coronary artery, high blood pressure, high cholesterol. I couldn't leave the house or even walk 100 meters. Not anymore. I help on the farm, ride horses, do everything. Before, I was like the walking dead. Now I'm just fine."

One man holding X-ray photographs up to the camera says, "Before giving birth, my wife's ultrasound showed that the baby had a dilated bladder and kidneys, that he would need an operation and might lose his kidneys. We came directly to Dr. Fritz, who treated him, and now he is cured and doesn't need an operation. God bless Dr. Fritz!"

In his medical office, Neuci Goncalves, MD displays the results of medical examinations, saying, "This is an exam to show breast cancer, called CA15.3. The first test shows 139 units, while normal is under 30. Six months after Dr. Fritz's treatments, the patient's new exam shows a drop from 139 to 25 units, within normal. So this is scientific, material proof that this spiritual treatment is effective."

I had been wondering how Rubens, who was a computer engineer, discovered this ability to channel Dr. Fritz's spirit. Were there signs when he was a child? These questions were resolved most dramatically by an interview with Rubens' mother and sister. His mother remembers things that happened even before Rubens was born: "When I was three or four months pregnant, I woke up one night and saw a boy this tall [gesturing with her hands], all in blue, with very curly blond hair, carrying firewood on his shoulders. He said, 'You are going to have a boy and he's going to be very different.'"

Rubens' sister speaks about their childhood. "He loved to take my dolls and open them. He said he was doing surgery, cutting with scissors, removing their heads, opening the heads. He liked doing this and said that I was his assistant." His mother also recalls Rubens' hobby: "He'd cut the little fingers, the little stomach, open up the dolls, a kind of obsession. Funny, I guess he did it because the dolls didn't bleed."

Rubens himself speaks about his childhood: "You know, as a kid, I had imaginary friends…chatting, telling stories, what I would do someday. My mother thought I was going crazy. And also my mother tells the story that I liked to run and jump over things. I remember jumping—boom—then nothing. I'd come back an hour later, an hour and a half later." Rubens' mother spoke of other episodes: "Until he was ten or eleven years old, he'd see people, talk with them. One man he spoke with a lot. Sometimes he'd call to me at night, 'Come here mother. Come here. He is talking to me.' He said he was keeping him company, protecting him. Besides headaches, Rubens had amnesia. I thought he was sick. I took him to some very well-known doctors who did lots of tests in the hospital. One of the doctors said to me, 'Your son has nothing wrong. He has a case of highly accentuated spirituality.'"

In the video, Rubens explains how he discovered his psychic ability. Reminiscing about his life as an engineer after graduating from a college of technology, he says: "In 1983, I was recently married and my wife was a Spiritist. One day, she said to me, 'Let's go to my friend's house for a Spiritist meeting.' I wasn't a Spiritist, but you know, when you are married, you'll do anything. So I went. I got there, sat down, and the praying started. Then she said, 'Come here, Rubens. Sit at the table with us to talk about Spiritism.' I said, 'Okay.' The minute I sat there, I started to get dizzy, nauseated, cold and hot flashes. I think I fainted, but I'm still not sure. I came back after forty minutes and the friend's daughter had a bunch of towels on her face. I awoke kind of dizzy and asked 'What happened?' Everybody looked at me quietly. She said, 'A spirit doctor came and operated on my daughter using a razor blade.' I looked at the bloody razor on the table and said I couldn't believe it was me that did that. 'No, it was really you.' A few days later, she went to the doctor, who said she had a fantastic operation for her cataracts and they were no longer there."

Rubens was certain then that he had been chosen by Dr. Fritz's spirit. He began studying Spiritism, Transcendental Psychology, and Umbanda in order to understand what had happened to him. But he couldn't find his answer in the physical environment. It is an answer he could find only by getting deeply into his metaphysical environment.

In the video, Rubens says, "The most crucial moment was when my ten-day-old adopted daughter arrived in a very weak condition. One of her lungs had atrophied, and she had no strength to suck milk. I had to wake up every hour to give her a teaspoon of milk. One of those days, I awoke at dawn. I had missed one of her feedings, gave her some milk, and I cried some. Then I asked Dr. Fritz, 'For the love of God, please help my sick little girl. She could die, and I need her alive.' I was at the side of her crib and saw a bright white light and his image. He looked at me and said that he would save my daughter to prove to me that God exists and that I would have to work for the sake of humanity. I said I'd do anything if he'd save my little girl, who had a really bad problem with her lungs and stomach. He asked me to place my hand on the baby's chest, and he saved my daughter. I remember that the next week I took her to the doctors, who were surprised because her lungs were healthy, nothing wrong. So I had no other choice. I let go of everything—engineering, my career, and my business—and decided to follow this path until today."

For the next few years, Rubens had to work five days a week as an engineer to support his family, and treat patients as Dr. Fritz on weekends. More recently, he has been able to work full-time as Dr. Fritz. He has treated some 350,000 patients since then. Almost every time Dr. Fritz opens his mouth, he speaks like this: "I touch the soul, not the flesh. Imagine if I worked every day, every hour, nonstop. I could cure only one thousandth of humanity. But if I cure 100 on the spiritual level, this will really spread."

Rubens also talks about Dr. Fritz's mission: "I think that this part of Fritz's mission is to make people understand a new concept of life, for them to really live. Krishnamurti said, 'There's a great difference between living and experiencing life.' Fritz wants you to experience your life, so that you can create new guidelines for your life—for why you're living. You can live eighty years and not know how to live those eighty years. There are ten-year-old children who've suffered much more than those eighty-year-olds and already know how to live."

One of the most impressive things about the Dr. Fritz phenomenon is that there are no mistakes in the treatments given and no sterilization of the medical instruments used in the abandoned warehouse. As Eduardo said, there has not been a single report of an in-house contagion or inflammation. Rubens speaks about this with self-confidence: "Our margin of error here is zero. There have been no proven cases of hospital infection, inflammation, clinical errors, nothing. It doesn't exist here. When a patient is treated here, we ask for the before and after exams, and they have to come back at least two weeks after the operation for follow-up on their case. A hospital infection can't happen here because God won't let you get a disease. He only cures. Here the spiritual forces are able to use some sort of energy for sterilization."

Dr. Fritz also explains about operating without anesthesia: "I don't use material medicine. I use astral medicine. I'm using my spiritual energy, and if you make a map of the brain waves, you'll see that mine and the patient's are very close, the same frequency. That is the theta wave. Then I can promote the liberation of chemical substances in the patient's own body, known as neuro-transmitters, or specifically, endorphins. And faith is a very important factor here. Faith has a mystical esoteric aspect and an energy aspect. When you are able to use this latter aspect, you liberate more endorphins and dopamines. All of these chemical compounds accelerate the higher energy state in your head."

In the video, David asks Rubens about communicating with Dr. Fritz, and Rubens explains: "I hear his voice and see him at night, mainly when he wants to say something, give me some advice. His world is spiritual. I don't know how I get there, but I know where I am. I'm okay, safe, calm. I'm not afraid. One day he was operating and was finished with everybody. My wife told him he was done, but he said, 'No, I am not finished.' She asked, 'Who's still left?' He said, 'He is. Rubens.' He had me lie on the operating table with a doctor at the side to assist. He said he was going to remove the cancer. I'd feel nothing, no bleeding, no prob-lems. He removed the skin cancer with no problems. Later, when I regained consciousness I was really pissed off because he hadn't warned me at all and I don't like operations. I saw the gauze and said, 'What's all this?' 'Remember what you had?' 'Yes. So?' 'He took it away,' and I saw the surgery scar and that was all. It took eleven years for him to do something for me physically."

~

Let's take a look at Dr. Fritz's history. According to investigators, Dr. Fritz was born in Munich, Germany. He studied medical science in Poland, became a military doctor, and died in a grenade explosion at Estonia in 1915 during World War I. The first person to channel Dr. Fritz's spirit was a young, uneducated farmer named Zé Arigó. One day in 1947, Arigó began having violent seizures, speaking German, and writing prescriptions for effective medicines for sick people. Then, in 1950, he performed an unexpected surgery on a senator who was a friend of his, removing a cancerous tumor from his lung using a rusty knife and dull scissors.

The operation was successful, and the news traveled rapidly throughout Brazil. After that, Arigó treated several hundred thousand patients but was eventually charged by the board of medical affairs with practicing medicine without a license. He was pardoned by Brazil's President Kubitschek, but later charged again, while Kubitschek was out of the country, and sentenced to eight months in jail. The local police refused to arrest Arigó and the prison warden also refused to have him imprisoned, but Arigó voluntarily went to jail. After a few days, sick people began lining up outside the prison for treatment, and Arigó continued to treat them. Eventually he was freed from prison with the support of Kubitschek, whose daughter he later treated.

In 1971, Arigó was killed instantly in a traffic accident. However, he had been warned by Dr. Fritz a month before that he would die. Dr. Fritz had given him a vision of a black cross. According to the book entitled *The Surgeon of the Rusty Knife*, by John G. Fuller, Arigó went to President Kubitschek and told him, "I don't want to have to tell you this, but I am going to die unnaturally, Mr. President." Kubitschek was surprised and confused, and said, "It's a joke, isn't it?" But Arigó shook his head and repeated in a sad voice, "I am sure I will die soon. It is very clear. This is a sorrowful moment, but I would like to say farewell. I believe that I will not meet you again, sir."

Following Arigó, the next person to channel Dr. Fritz's spirit was a man named Oscar Wilde, who began channeling in 1975. Oscar operated using a knife without anesthesia, just as Arigó had.

Dr. Rudolf Passian and Dr. Kronel from West Germany investigated Wilde's treatments and confirmed their effectiveness. Wilde was also accused of violating medical laws but was judged not guilty.

After working hard for many years as Dr. Fritz, Wilde also was killed instantly in a traffic accident. After that, Wilde's younger brother, named Edvaldo, began channeling Dr. Fritz's spirit and treating sick people. Strangely, a few years later, Edvaldo also died instantly in a traffic accident. Then, in 1980, a gynecologist, Dr. Edson Queiroz, became Dr. Fritz's channeler. As Dr. Fritz, Dr. Queiroz performed surgery on 13,848 patients in three years, treating them all for free. Then, in what seems a cruel fate for Dr. Fritz's channelers, Dr. Queiroz died instantly when he was stabbed by a former staff person.

It is a frightening fact that Rubens already knows the date of his own unusual and unnatural death. Rubens says, "Dr. Fritz has given me four years and nine months more to live [until around December of the year 2000]. It was complicated at the beginning, because I didn't understand anything. When he gave me this deadline, I immediately told him I'd never work with him again. But that didn't work and I went back. It was really tough at the beginning, because he was giving me a period to live, when I will die, why, where, how. I just don't know who is going to do this.

"It's really complicated, a psychological shock, you know, with my daughter, trying to live my life. I went into a violent depression, because I believe in what he says, since I believe in what he does. You know, if there's a person who has impeccable behavior, always makes you certain, you have to believe everything. It's impossible that he could be lying. I also know he's not talking nonsense because he gave this period to live to all the other mediums—Arigó, Wilde, Queiroz, Edvaldo. It was difficult. One day he said to me, 'You don't have a time to die, you have a time to live. You have to learn how to live during these years you have. If you know how to do that, you will have a better understanding of what you're doing and who you are.'

"This is my last time here," Dr. Fritz says. "It is an incredible opportunity. I am no longer afraid of death, because I'm sure that when this happens, my daughter will be proud to remember that her father saved and helped thousands of people. And I will feel calm about this death because I will have done my duty, fulfilled my mission. To live this way, you can differentiate between simply living without knowing why and being here on earth with an objective, not for you to be selfish about this objective, but for you to benefit others."

But Rubens' wife, Rita, feels differently about it: "I think it's unfair. How could this be? I don't question God, but why this for someone who does good for so many others? Rubens leaves home to treat people who he's never met before, doesn't know. What kind of mission is this that he has to be taken away? I dream a lot, can't stop thinking about that day, this stuff about his death, and I'm really scared. I wake up frightened to see if he's still lying by me. He seems to be resigned to this, but I can't accept it."

You can call it fate, but it's still a very rough way to live.

As I sat watching the video, I began considering going back to Rio de Janeiro to do some research. Then I would be able to write about this phenomenon and introduce Dr. Fritz's message to mankind, so that perhaps readers could get some kind of inspiration, as I did. One scene near the end of the video finally convinced me to go back. The music from my CD *Childhood Dream* played over the scenes of the ups and downs in Arigó's life. I was very grateful that David had used my music for this very touching sequence, and I felt as if I was linked to Dr. Fritz's spirit through the sound of my music. My decision was confirmed when I saw in the final credits, "Music by Masao Maki."

As soon as I successfully concluded my business in Japan, I would go see Dr. Fritz again.

TYPHOON OF SYNCHRONICITY

November 9

Lately, I had begun to think that everything that happened to me had some message in it, that every incident had meaning. Every time something occurred with synchronous good timing, I felt like I was getting closer to the energy of the universe. This trip to Japan was full of such coincidences. I've had so much of this phenomenon in my life that some of my friends have nicknamed me the "Walking Typhoon of Synchronicity."

On this trip, it began on the plane. I was flying on Japan Airlines from San Francisco to Narita. I had drunk too much coffee to fall asleep, so I was working on one of my regular columns for a Japanese New Age magazine. Just as I was writing the lines "In Boulder, I ran the Bolder Boulder, a 10K marathon. Yuko Arimori ran the same marathon," a stewardess brought me a stack of newspapers. I hadn't read a Japanese paper for a long time, so I picked one up from the stack, put down my pen, and opened it at random. My eyes immediately fell on the lines "I like to run with Yuko Arimori." Instantly, my attention was captured. Yuko Arimori is a famous Japanese runner who won the silver medal in the Barcelona Olympics and the bronze medal in the Atlanta Olympics. The author continued, "In Boulder, Colorado, there is a 10K marathon called the Bolder Boulder...." It was nearly the same thing I had just written in my article. I felt the coincidence was a good sign for me to start my new project in Japan.

When I visited my home town in Oita City, where my family

lives, I experienced a continuous wave of synchronicity nearly every day. For example: On my first day in Oita, I went with my family to dine at a new Chinese restaurant on the hill. When we opened the door, the owner yelled, "Wow! Maki-san!" We used to play in a rock and roll band together almost twenty years before. I had been hoping to run into him somewhere. It was a great surprise for me, because I had no idea he owned a Chinese restaurant now.

On the second day, I made an appointment to meet a couple of friends. While waiting in the lobby of my hotel, I looked at the dining room's display of blowfish dishes, thinking, "I haven't eaten blowfish for years. I'd really like to have some today." When my friends showed up, they took me to a fancy new restaurant nearby called Fukutei, which specializes in blowfish dishes.

On the third day, a woman from a newspaper treated me to dinner at a very small gourmet restaurant. While we sat munching the fine food and drinking the finest sake, the owner/chef came to speak with us. "Sir, I hear you came from the United States," she said. "I have a girlfriend in Colorado."

"That's a coincidence," I said. "I live in Colorado too, in a town called Boulder."

"What?" she said. "My friend lives there also. She's married to the owner of a sushi bar."

"Really?" I said. "What's the name of the sushi bar?"

"I think the name is Sushi Zanmai and her husband's name is Nao." "Sushi Zanmai is my restaurant, and Nao-san is my partner!" I exclaimed. Of course, the woman from the newspaper was quite surprised.

On my fourth day in Japan, I had a lunch date with a high school buddy who works at city hall. The day before, I had seen a curry shop called Salnato and had thought how much I would like to go there. As my friend and I were walking through town, he asked, "What would you like to eat for lunch?" I don't know why, but the answer that came from my mouth was, "Whatever. I'll leave it to you."

"Okay," he said. "I know a great, tasty curry shop nearby. I've been going there for ten years." And he brought me to Salnato.

On the fifth day, I went to a karaoke box, a private room where anyone can have a party and sing karaoke. It was the first time I had ever been to one in Japan. I got really drunk and decided that, out of the more than 5,000 tunes in the request book, I wanted to sing a song called "Linda Linda." I pushed the number of the song, and before anything was visible on the large TV screen, a woman sitting across the table suddenly yelled, "Oh no, Maki-san. I have a feeling you're going to sing 'Linda Linda'!" Two seconds later, the title came up on the screen and everyone was shocked because I had never sung the song before and there was no way she could have guessed I would pick that song from among the 5,000 choices.

When timing and coincidences go together like this, it seems that everything goes smoother and better. Friends attract friends and luck attracts luck, and that's why in Tokyo I got signed to a contract to release my CD *Childhood Dream* on the biggest New Age label in Japan. Then I signed a contract with a major Japanese publisher to publish the manuscript about my adventures in Peru, called *The Trip to the Magical Incas*. In addition, I landed a contract with a comic book publisher in Japan for the comic book version of my autobiography, *The Rock 'n' Roll Sushi Chef Story*.

My success with these three big projects seemed like an auspicious sign to go back to Brazil right away to see Dr. Fritz. I had finished up everything in Japan two weeks ahead of schedule, so I decided to stop over in San Francisco to confer with the publisher about some editing on my debut book in English, *Spiritual Adventures of a Sushi Chef*. I stayed at my friend Kaori's apartment. She is a professional transpersonal astrologer and the co-author of my past two Japanese books.

"Maki-san, do you remember what day November 8 is?" She asked me.

"No," I said. "What is it?"

"Two years ago today, we debunked the hoax about the prophetic Indian leaves of Agasthya. Then last year on this day we debunked the big lie of the shaman of the Incas at Machu Picchu."

It was true, I realized, but I hadn't even planned to be at her home until just recently.

"I really think this has to have some meaning in it," she said.

The next day I woke up really late, due to jet lag. Kaori was watching the Dr. Fritz video I had brought with me. She asked, "Maki-san, is it okay if I go to Rio de Janeiro with you?"

"But I thought you had to write your Ph.D. dissertation!"

"I can do it after I come back. Right now I have a problem I would really like Dr. Fritz to cure."

"But I don't even know who Dr. Fritz is," I said, "I can't guarantee he can cure you."

"That's okay," she replied. "I'd just like to give it a try. It'll be like a vacation for me. Don't take it too seriously. But these symptoms after my car accident…none of the doctors or alternative healers I've consulted have been able to cure them. See? You can touch it." She showed me the vertebra on the back of her neck. I felt a swelling, and it looked very painful.

Two years before, Kaori and I had gone to India for a month and exposed the scams going on there, and one year before we went from Cuzco to Machu Picchu and debunked the scam of the fake shaman of the Incas. Now we were going to Rio together at the exact same time. Were we going to debunk the Dr. Fritz phenomenon as well?

DISCOVERY OF THE DISCOVERY CHANNEL

November 25

Having caught the midnight flight from Miami, Kaori and I arrived at the Rio de Janeiro airport at seven o'clock in the morning. This time, I had arranged our travel plans as carefully as I could. We made our reservations through a tour company that specialized in South American travel and were met at the airport by a tour guide. We would be staying in a five-star beachfront hotel on Copacabana Beach at a special tour rate of less than half price.

I knew that dining out would be too expensive and that it would be difficult to maintain my low-sodium, loosely vegetarian diet, so we brought cooking pans, rice, miso, and soy sauce with us. However, despite our careful preparations, nothing went according to plan. But that's part of the fun of traveling in countries like Brazil.

We arrived at the hotel sleepy and jet-lagged, but no rooms were ready, so we had to wait four hours on a couch in the lobby. Finally the hotel staff took us to an old-fashioned room on the seventeenth floor. It seemed unusually dark. Upon closer inspection, I found that the glass door to the verandah had been broken and temporarily replaced with a big plywood board. I was somewhat nonplussed. After all, this was a five-star hotel and the tallest (thirty floors) on Copacabana Beach! So I went back to the lobby to negotiate another room. Finally, they reluctantly gave us a new room, and Kaori fell asleep on the bed the moment she lay down. I myself was so excited about seeing Dr. Fritz that I took a shower to get over my own sleepiness and hailed a taxi to the old warehouse.

I arrived a little after noon. Right away I noticed some improvements since I had visited half a year ago. Big fluorescent lights and several fans had been installed in the ceiling of the large hall. And the hundreds of patients who before had stood for nearly the whole day, now had brand-new, white, metal folding chairs to sit on. Feeling nostalgic, I walked into the main clinic room. There I saw a crew of Americans preparing to shoot some film. The last time I was there a local TV crew had paid a visit, but these people had brand-new equipment and the staff seemed very professional and refined. A Caucasian woman in her thirties with short hair was taking notes. She appeared to be the director, so I walked over to her and asked, "Did you folks come from the United States?"

With no trace of annoyance on her face, she answered "Yes! We were sent by the Discovery Channel. We've been here ten days now. Today is our last day of filming and tomorrow we're returning to the States."

The Discovery Channel, with its fascinating science documentaries and programs, is my favorite channel on cable TV. The director told me: "Among the various spirit healers, I think Rubens—or Dr. Fritz—has the most advanced technology in the modern world. We've been able to shoot plenty of astonishing, significant footage. We're all very satisfied with our visit."

I left the clinic room and went to the walkway, trying to stay out of the way of the film crew. Then I saw Rubens and his wife walking into the large hall, welcomed with applause from all the patients. Rubens was walking quickly towards the operating room, but on the way he noticed me standing there and came over and shook my hand. "I'm glad you could come back again," he said. "Feel free to come and go as you please here." I was flattered that he still remembered me. As I shook his hand, I got a good look at him. I noticed that he was wearing a tiny earring in his left ear. It was cute.

A few minutes later, Rubens changed out of his T-shirt and into a white coat. Two huge spotlights shone on him as he sat in front of his little desk. While the big camera filmed, Rubens again put his right hand over both eyes and quickly fell into his trance.

I recalled how David's video answered my questions about Rubens' experience of connecting with Dr. Fritz: "When he arrives," Rubens said in the video, "he takes over my body. The feeling is like entering a cold pool, with my whole body gradually submerging up to the top until nothing is left...and poof...then he comes and works. I feel like I've gone to some place like a tunnel, and at the end of the tunnel is a strong light. But it's a good feeling, not bad. I feel calm. Every time he comes I see myself leaving my body and rising above. I'm up here, and my body's down there. I can't see Dr. Fritz. What I see is a strong light that enters my body, gluing to my body. Then I go away, farther and farther."

Dr. Fritz spoke about his experience of entering Rubens' body as well: "When I enter his body, it's unpleasant because it's a small body. Not just him—any body is small. To have the material hold this energy, you have to mold one to the other, to join his brain-wave frequency to mine, and to do this quickly. That's why he falls like this, dizzy. It's like another person taking you over. You leave, another enters, and you lose your identity."

Spiritists describe this phenomenon of spirits and human beings coming together as "incorporating." In their book *Healing States*, co-authors Dr. Stanley Krippner Ph.D. and co-author Alberto Villoldo, Ph.D., who studied Edson Queiroz, Dr. Fritz's previous channeler, write: "[Queiroz's] ability to diagnose and perform surgery rapidly may be an example of state-dependent learning, a condition in which people can learn a task while drugged or hypnotized that they cannot perform in ordinary consciousness. However, they can recall the task and perform it again when they reenter the altered state....State-dependent learning also characterizes many cases of multiple-personality disorders, a condition in which an individual manifests two or more distinct personalities....Each subpersonality, when dominant, determines that person's attitudes, showing relatively distinct behavioral patterns....In the case of mediumistic incorporation, the spirit appears to facilitate the functioning of the medium. Rather than being conceived as an instance of multiple-personality disorder, the relationship between Queiroz and Dr. Fritz can better be described as a case of what psychologists often call co-consciousness, in which more than one consciously experiencing psychological entity can exist within a healthy human organism. Each personality has some sense of its own identity or selfhood despite their relatively separate and discrete identifications."

Brazilian psychologist Dr. Gilda Moura, who has researched Rubens and the Dr. Fritz phenomenon extensively, explained this point in a more comprehensive way. "One of the basic questions is the difference between mediumship and multiple personalities. In other words, in the manifestations of different personalities, one of the principal factors is control. The medium has control in these manifestations. He is not absorbed by this influence or by the archetypal images or by another's access to another level of reality or information. He has the control to enter and leave. This is the big difference between a schizophrenic and a mystic. That is, both are in the same ocean, but the mystic knows how to swim while the schizophrenic drowns."

Under the bright lights and microphones of the film crew, Dr. Fritz had already finished operating on a few patients without any difficulty. Then came the last big operation of the day, on an older woman, who had a serious brain tumor. Standing next to me, the director from the Discovery Channel whispered into my ear, "This is the most difficult operation of the day. I heard this woman has been told by all the doctors in major hospitals that it is too late to do anything about her brain tumor."

First, Dr. Fritz shaved off the hair just above her right ear. Then, without anesthesia, as usual, he cut into the skin with a scalpel, tapping it with the handle of another stainless steel knife. I watched as he made a three-inch incision above her ear. Speaking in English, he said, "Now I'm going to make a hole in the skull here. Please give me the electric drill." His assistant handed Dr. Fritz something like a dentist's drill, only a lot larger.

He put the drill bit into the three-inch incision and began drilling into the woman's skull. At both sides of her bed two young men stood wearing very anxious expressions. I learned that they were the woman's sons. One assisted by taping a nozzle from an electric pump near the area where Dr. Fritz drilled, in order to suck up the blood. I learned that he was the younger son and that he was a pediatrician by profession.

As the hole was being drilled in her skull, the patient spoke in a faint voice to her sons. As far as I could see, she showed no signs of pain. The film crew stood close to Dr. Fritz near the patient's head and I stood near her feet, so I couldn't see inside her skull. Dr. Fritz took a very long hypodermic needle, about five to seven inches long, and pushed it into her brain through the hole he had just drilled. As he drew back the plunger on the syringe, it filled up with something, and I wondered if it was the cancer molecules or a part of the brain tumor. The sons were holding their mother's hands and appeared to be praying.

As Dr. Fritz extracted this material from the woman's brain, he said something to her, and she raised her right leg. After he said something else, she raised her left leg. I noticed that on her rather large feet she was wearing very cute, pink, flowered socks. The fingernails on her hands, which were being so tightly held by her sons, were manicured and painted with bright, red polish. Suddenly, somehow, I felt lighter about the operation.

Her operation lasted longer than anyone else's. Most of Dr. Fritz's operations take about five minutes, but he spent nearly twenty minutes working on her. As soon as he finished, he went directly to the large hall and began injecting the few hundred patients there. About twenty minutes later, the two sons were being interviewed by the Discovery Channel director in the parking lot. At first, they merely described the procedure, but near the end of the interview, the older brother suddenly burst into tears and began speaking in awkward English with great passion and emotion.

"I have a message to deliver to everybody in the world. In this Dr. Fritz clinic, there is the love of God vividly alive. I believe in God, and I also believe in Dr. Fritz. He is giving the operation to my mother without any further charges. The things happening here is not magic and not superstitions. Here every day the authentic miracle is happening." At moments he halted to search for the right English words, and his younger brother, the doctor, helped him. It was very moving.

Then, to my surprise, their mother, who had just had brain surgery, walked over to where they stood, accompanied by her daughter. I thought, "It can't be!" but when I saw the cotton gauze bandage above her ear where she had been shaved, I knew it was her. I thought, "This is remarkable. Some kind of medical revolution is going on here."

The interviewer began speaking with the mother, holding the microphone for her. Unfortunately, I couldn't understand Portuguese, so I walked over to the two sons and introduced myself. I asked them if I could interview them the following night. The younger brother said, "Yes, please. If you can come to my house tomorrow night, that would be the most convenient." He wrote down the address and phone number.

Back under the new fluorescent lights in the large hall, Dr. Fritz was still working on hundreds of patients, jumping from one to another, vaccinating them with his miracle injections. Suddenly, I felt exhausted. This wasn't surprising, since I hadn't had any sleep since leaving the United States the previous morning. Fortunately, the staff of the Discovery Channel offered me a ride to my hotel in their van. At the hotel, as I was wishing them good-bye, the director said, "The Dr. Fritz phenomenon went far beyond our expectations. It was a real discovery for us."

When I got back to my room, I didn't even have enough energy to take a shower before I crashed on the bed.

November 26

I slept like mud. Just before I dozed off, Kaori asked me what time I was going to get up in the morning. I remember answering, "I haven't slept for a long time. Let's wake up when we wake up." When I finally awoke and looked at my wristwatch, it was two thirty in the afternoon.

Of course, we were both quite hungry, so we checked the room service menu. We were shocked. A shrimp cocktail appetizer cost forty-five U.S. dollars. That was more than twice as expensive as in the United States. We vowed that we would never order anything from the hotel, even if we were starving. While Kaori showered, I found a store in Copacabana, bought a portable electric stove, and brought it back to the room. We washed the rice in the bathroom and cooked rice and miso soup, a simple Japanese meal. It was healthful and tasty, and we were very glad we had brought these supplies to Brazil with us. After our late brunch, we took a taxi to Dr. Fritz's clinic.

By the time we arrived, it was dark. Inside the clinic, Kaori was fascinated by everything she heard and saw. She reminded me of myself when I first arrived there half a year ago. "These rotten, scraped walls!" she exclaimed. "To me they are like the walls of the most beautiful temples in Japan. And when I see the patients waiting in long lines, I feel the same spirituality I felt in Hindu ashrams in India." She was very excited and high. I told her to calm down. "This is just the beginning. Let's go out and have something to drink."

We walked out the gate to the spot where the vendors were lined up. One young lady was efficiently peeling a mango, so we ordered a mango juice. Soon, a young, intelligent-looking woman came up to us and said in clear, crisp English, "Excuse me. This man really wants to talk with you folks." Behind her stood a stocky, middle-aged man.

I recognized their faces. The young Brazilian woman was one of Dr. Fritz's nurses. All day yesterday she had been at Dr. Fritz's side. The man was also a hospital volunteer. Yesterday I had seen him giving a long speech to the patients in the large hall. His voice was very strong and the patients listened eagerly. It was a sight to behold. The young woman said, "My name is Alice. I'm an English teacher, but on Monday and Tuesday I work here as a volunteer. Now I am going to translate for Sergio."

The man loved to talk, and his face lit up at the prospect of speaking with us. "My name is Sergio," he said. "I'm fifty-two years old. As you can see, I'm a very rough, macho man, and since I was young I have fought a lot and hurt many people. But last year I got malignant sarcoma—a tumor on both shoulders—and the doctors said they would have to cut off both my arms. Even then, they said, there was only a slim chance of my survival. I was desperate. Some of my friends told me about Dr. Fritz. I had no other choice. I was willing to try anything to save my life and my arms. Dr. Fritz examined me and told me that he could operate, but that this is a rather difficult disease, so I had to believe in the existence of the spirit within me, otherwise it wouldn't be healed. Then he operated twice on the right shoulder and three times on the left shoulder."

Sergio took off the T-shirt he was wearing and showed off the scars from the operations. I saw scars about three inches long in five different places on his shoulders. "Dr. Fritz gave me instruction every time he operated," he continued. "He said 'Don't be violent and short-tempered. You have to become a person who thinks of other people's benefit first. Otherwise this disease won't be cured.' So I prayed with all my soul every morning and every night. Then, miraculously, I was completely healed. The doctors who examined me in the big hospital were very surprised and called it a miracle.

"But it wasn't just my body and disease that was cured. The cure happened in my spirit, too. Until then, I hated people and I was jealous and always fighting. Now my heart and spirit have been totally reborn. Now I'm happy for the first time in my life. That's why I like to talk about my experience and pass on this message to others. That's why I'm working here as a volunteer. I want you to tell the story of my healed spirit also."

Kaori and I were pretty impressed as we drank our juice.

After talking with Sergio, Kaori and I took a taxi to our eight o'clock appointment with the brothers. Their apartment was in a building surrounded by an iron security fence. Of course, the door was locked. The younger brother welcomed us and took us up to the third floor, where we met his mother again. I thought with amazement, "She just had brain surgery last night!" Yet there she was, sitting at the dining room table sipping some soup. She was very kind and polite to us. The young men's father and grandfather also came to welcome us and ushered us into the living room. Then the younger brother brought out X-ray photos of his mother's brain scan and explained, "Dr. Fritz took out this part, this shadow here, completely. We couldn't see it with this X-ray, but Dr. Fritz also discovered that the cancer has already spread to other parts of her brain. He is going to decide next Monday if he needs to do another operation."

Eventually, I asked him the question that was uppermost in my mind. "You are a recognized and respected doctor at a hospital. Why would you leave your mother's fate to Dr. Fritz, someone who doesn't even have a medical education or license?"

"If my mom had a simpler disease," he said, "then I could treat her, or the hospital I work for could cure her without any problem. But the cancer cells have already spread, so even using the most modern medical techniques, it is almost impossible to cure her. That was the hospital's diagnosis. I had been hearing about Dr. Fritz for a long time, but when my mother became sick, I went to the clinic myself many times and checked with my own eyes what he was doing. I reconfirmed a lot of the examples of perfect cures myself. I have come to the conclusion that Dr. Fritz is the only chance my mother has to survive her illness."

I discovered that he was not a conventional, narrow-minded Western medical doctor. After we talked for a while, he told us he had read the Portuguese version of *The Celestine Prophecy* and had been very impressed by it. Then he told us about his astrological chart, and since Kaori is a professional astrologer, she spent some time going over it with him. He was very impressed with her explanations. We were only supposed to visit for half an hour, but we spent more than two enjoyable hours talking about a variety of topics.

Just before we left, I went to his mother's room to say goodbye. She was watching television with her daughter, and we took some photos of them. Then she kissed me on both cheeks. It was very sweet. I prayed hard for her complete recovery and was again moved by the work Dr. Fritz has been doing with all different kinds of people.

When we got back to the hotel, Kaori and I ate the leftovers from our lunch, cooking the rice with vegetables into a porridge. Kaori said, "I really want to get treated for my problem, so tomorrow morning we're going to get up really early to get a good place in line."

"Way to go, Kaori," I said, and set the alarm clock.

Kaori's Astral Body Injection

November 27

Somehow, neither of us made it up early on the fourth day of our visit to Rio. When we finally crawled out of bed, we cooked our breakfast in the hotel room and then took a taxi to Dr. Fritz's clinic, arriving around eleven in the morning.

When I had been there half a year before, I had seen the staff collecting money from patients by passing around something similar to a church donation box. Since then, they had built a simple window where they collected fees. The day before, Alice, the volunteer nurse and English teacher, told me, "We use about 8,000 cotton bandages a day, in addition to all the syringes, operating tools, rent, electricity, and so on. It's really hard to manage a hospital this large."

During the television interviews the other day, a worker explained how the money was being spent, using graphs and such. It was not my job to audit the hospital, so I decided not to worry about it too much.

Kaori paid about $10 and received a piece of paper with the number 646. That meant that 645 patients were already waiting their turn to see Dr. Fritz. But we had arrived prepared to wait in line the whole day, so we didn't really mind getting such a high number.

In the large hall, a middle-aged woman was speaking into a microphone about her healing experience with Dr. Fritz. Afterwards, an older nurse led the group in prayer. There are different prayers said here, I suppose, but I found a flier that had a prayer printed on it, and I got someone to translate it into English for me. It went like this:

Here comes the spirit of Dr. Fritz,
The German doctor with the sublime mission of passing on joy and bringing happiness
Through healing the illnesses of our brothers of any religion.

And in the name of Jesus,
He comes to heal the sick ones, from children to the elderly,
Spreading his benign light and preaching Jesus's words.

Blessed be Dr. Fritz!
He comes to fulfill his beautiful mission in the name of the beloved Jesus,
And to heal each and every one of our brothers.

We thank God and Jesus,
For such a happy moment,
For the grace of this divine light,
Through the blessed Dr. Fritz.

Watching hundreds of patients praying so sincerely was very moving. The vibration was holy, but it didn't seem as though Dr. Fritz was creating some new religious organization. My speculation is that he uses the name of Jesus, someone they are quite familiar with, in order to make people feel more comfortable and unthreatened. In the video Rubens says, "Everybody can have the religion they want. I think that in a few years, in the near future, there won't be any religion at all. How can I say that? More and more people are seeking or trying to be in contact with God, and they will realize that they don't need a church or temple for that. I think that what I do and what other mediums who cure or do materialization are showing is, 'Look, people, there is something here. Learn with this here.'"

Dr. Fritz says that waiting all day long for one's turn to be treated is part of the spiritual learning process. Before they have to wait this way, a lot of patients think to themselves, "Why me? Why is it only me who has to suffer this much?" That is egoistic thinking, Dr. Fritz says. After having to wait all day and watching patients all around them suffering more than themselves, they may change their thinking and learn to pray, "These people are suffering more than me, God, and I can be treated later. Please treat them first and ease their suffering." Thus, waiting provides an opportunity to develop one's compassion for others.

While Kaori and I were drinking vegetable soup from a paper cup given to us by the workers, Rubens and his wife came into the hospital. As usual, spontaneous applause broke out in the hall. Before he changed from his T-shirt into a white smock, I introduced him to Kaori. She showed Rubens her paper, with the number 646 written on it, and said, "Later on, I will get a treatment from Dr. Fritz." But Rubens smiled and said, "Oh, we can ignore the number on this paper. I'm sure that Dr. Fritz can treat you as the very first patient." Kaori protested, "Oh no. This is part of my learning experience, so I'm going to wait in line just like the others." We all laughed. Within a few minutes, Rubens had changed into his white smock, removed his eyeglasses, and begun channeling Dr. Fritz.

That day, three surgeons from one of the big hospitals in Rio de Janeiro were present to observe and assist with the operations. In the operating room, Dr. Fritz began by cutting into the first patient's abdomen. He worked incredibly fast, moving on to the next patient for a spine operation in about five minutes. After each operation, Dr. Fritz left the incision as it was, moved on to the next, and left the three visiting doctors to suture the incisions smoothly and precisely. Also on that day, a film crew from Teve TV Globo of Rio was filming the operations.

Soon Dr. Fritz began operating on a middle-aged black woman. He pushed some scissors into her back, near the spine, and squeezed them deep into her flesh. I saw her expression change rapidly, and she began moaning with pain. Dr. Fritz spoke softly into her ear and she nodded a few times. It was the first time

I had ever seen a patient suffer during an operation. Apparently, not all patients were completely free of pain. In a few moments, however, it appeared that the pain went away, and the woman began talking to the nurse as Dr. Fritz continued.

After Dr. Fritz had finished about ten patients, one of the doctors who was volunteering asked Dr. Fritz for a treatment. Dr. Fritz injected him with a hypodermic needle about three inches long. I watched as the needle went deeply into the man's arm, and after Dr. Fritz left the operating room, I went to the man and asked him about his experience. "This is the third time I have come to observe and help as a volunteer," he said. "Dr. Fritz is a wonderful doctor with superhuman abilities."

I asked him if the injection with the long needle had been painful. "Oh no, no," he replied. "That's the strange thing. I didn't feel any pain. I have been suffering from rheumatoid arthritis for a few months and couldn't move my right arm well because of the numbness I felt there. But with Dr. Fritz's injections, it has gotten a lot better. Look at this." He opened and closed his right hand several times and said, "For those of us who have studied medical science, Dr. Fritz is a rare and fascinating being. I can learn a lot from him, so next week I'll be here again to help."

About ten of the patients whom Dr. Fritz had operated on had already put on their clothes and, without any assistance, simply set out for home. Since there was no place in the facility for them to stay, the patients simply left on foot or in their wheelchairs.

Now Kaori and I were the only ones remaining in the operating room. For some time, she looked like she had something she wanted to say to me. Now that she had the opportunity, her words came out seamlessly: "Wow, Maki-san! As I expected, Dr. Fritz is incredible! I was so moved. And these people who are volunteering here are so kind and devoted! Everyone in the operating room is relaxed and friendly and harmonious. I think that during operations in a regular hospital, people are very nervous because there is always such anxiety that the operation may fail and the patient may die. But here, under the guidance of Dr. Fritz's spirit, everyone feels that it is going to be all right, so they can smile while it's going on." As I listened to her, I felt that her perception and way of thinking were very close to my own.

For the next three hours, we waited like patient children. As we talked, I told her that I had heard Dr. Fritz treated one person and one disease at a time. If someone wanted to be cured of five or ten diseases at a time, they were expecting too much of him. It was about six o'clock, and Kaori's turn was approaching. She told me, "I would really like to be cured today of this problem I've had since the traffic accident." Again, she showed me the place on her neck, and as I touched it, I could see how swollen it was. It was even painful to look at.

Finally, her turn came, and I prepared to photograph the event. Kaori pointed to the back of her neck and explained her symptoms to Dr. Fritz. He said, "No problem," and after so many hours waiting, it was all over in the blink of an eye. We said, "*Obrigado*," and left the room. When we got to the gate of the warehouse, Kaori turned to me and said excitedly, "That wasn't painful at all. I don't think the needle even touched my skin. I think the brown liquid was just injected into the cotton gauze on top of my skin."

I thought so too. Perhaps it depended on the person and the symptoms. A half year before, when I got the injection in my left shoulder, I was sure I felt the liquid going into my body, and I watched many times as patients were injected in the back or neck and the liquid disappeared. But even if the needle didn't penetrate the bodies of some people, the treatment seemed to effect a cure. How could this be explained?

Dr. Fritz explains that he injects the energy body, called the astral body: "I see colors, diagnosis only, not treatment, just to see what the problem is. I can't see liver or heart or brain. I just see colors, like the chakras, the same system, but not the mystical principles. The mistake human beings make is that they just focus on the visible body. They forget that there is an invisible energy body. I see an array of colors that function like the density of water. It's like the phenomenon that happens with the formation of a rainbow. You human beings have to be able to see these energies.

You can call the energy body that is around the physical body any-thing you like. A name is just a name. Steiner called it the astral body. Steiner studied the principles of the astral body. So I am injecting into the astral body. So I am extracting the tumor first from the astral body and second from the material body. In the astral body, we don't have pain, bleeding, infections."

Dr. Fritz says that if people want to understand his ability, they need to study Rudolph Steiner's research. Steiner, born in Austria in the last century, created a huge body of work in an enormous range of disciplines: in education (his main field), bio-logy, and especially in medicine. He called his medical theory "anthroposophic medicine." It is still taught today at the Steiner center in Switzerland. According to Dr. Eleanor Luzes, who has extensively researched the Dr. Fritz phenomenon, Steiner pro-posed that doctors undergo an initiation in which they develop clairvoyance and a greater capacity for perception.

By treating the astral body, the infection in the material body disappears. Dr. Fritz tried to explain this phenomenon using the terminology of quantum physics: "The alcohol in the injection liquid is composed of carbon, hydrogen, and oxygen. It's easier to break down these molecules using the raw materials. In reality, the body is not solid. The body is the electromagnetic union of par-ticles in constant resonance. So when I inject this composition of iodine and alcohol, these substances take on a different configura-tion inside each person's body, making different substances. I move the magnetic fields. I can use these fields to stop the bleed-ing and pain and to increase or decrease the growth of cells. Energy fields and mass... You put together the mass; everything is mass. If you interrelate these and have the same frequency field, you generate the same magnetic field. You have to move the field to learn how to do this. That's all, but really it's the most difficult."

Dr. Fritz said it is difficult to manipulate the electromagnetic fields, but for me, just understanding quantum physics theory is very difficult. It was Kaori's astral body injection that raised my interest in these specialized subjects.

Kaori was still excited. She told me, "I'm really glad I came to see Dr. Fritz. I felt just like when I received *darshan* with Sai Baba. I didn't feel like I was getting treated by a doctor; I felt I was being blessed by God's energy."

Dr. Fritz had another big clinic in São Paulo, and we learned that in the next two days he was going to treat patients there. Since our main purpose for being in Brazil was to report on Dr. Fritz, we put São Paulo on our itinerary.

It was still early when we left the clinic and found a taxi, so we decided to visit a Spiritist church. That morning I had discovered a very interesting monthly magazine called *Curas Espirituais* (Spiritual Healing) at a newsstand. The cover of the magazine featured an attractive photo of Rubens as Dr. Fritz, holding his hands up and with a brilliant white light behind his head. Although I can't read Portuguese, I could tell from the pictures that there were many psychic surgeries being performed by channelers and mediums throughout Brazil. Of course, the layout about Dr. Fritz's work was the largest in the magazine—about ten pages of photos of his operations and the clinic—but besides Dr. Fritz, there were articles about other psychic healers. One church, called Frei Luis, named for the Spiritist doctor who founded it, was located in Rio de Janeiro, so we decided to visit it.

Spiritism originated with the Frenchman Alan Kardec, who wrote a book called *The Book of Spirits*. The book arrived from France last century and generated a new belief system in Brazil called Spiritism, or Kardecism. In France, it is a minor religion, but in Brazil, it spread widely. Spiritism describes an invisible world populated by spirits. Many of these spirits have a mission to come to the aid of those still on the material plane. Spiritists believe in karma and the healing power of spirits.

Frei Luis is less a church than a large spiritual commune. Located in the foothills of the mountains, the facilities include a chapel, hospitals, bookstores, a restaurant, and sleeping accommodations. It seemed as though the day we visited, Wednesday, was a special ceremonial day. Disciples—old and young, men and women—dressed in white shirts and pants, carried one flower (a marigold or gladiola) in each hand. They were walking around contemplatively or sitting underneath trees on benches and meditating.

As Kaori and I wandered around, we discovered about a hundred people lined up at the chapel's back door. I had an intimation that something interesting was going on there, so we pretended to be disciples and waited with the others, moving silently and slowly towards the door. When we finally arrived, we were asked to remove our shoes and wristwatches. As we proceeded along the walkway, I noticed familiar music coming from somewhere, and recognized it as the *Adagio* by Albinoni.

About half an hour later, shoes in hand, we were shown into a large strange room lit only by a dim red lamp. Inside, about twenty Spiritist healers were doing one-on-one healing sessions with disciples. I felt as though the big dark room was filled with entities from the spirit world. I was instantly happy, thinking, "Wow, great things must be happening here! Everyone is really into it!"

Soon I found myself standing in front of a young man who was more than six feet tall. He asked me to put my shoes on the floor, close my eyes, and relax. So I closed my eyes, and he moved both his hands from the tip of my head to my feet, without touching me, all the while making sounds like, "sshhh, sshhh, sshhh" and sending me a great amount of Chi energy. I don't know if I was feeling vibrations from the moving air or the Chi energy itself, but with my eyes closed, I felt it on the skin of whatever part of my body he was working on. When I opened my eyes slightly to sneak a peek, I found I was right each time. Gradually I started to feel very light and joyous and energetic. I thought, "This guy doesn't even know me and he isn't charging me anything but he's giving his all to heal me with his energy!" I felt very grateful.

The healing lasted about ten minutes, and then the healers switched to the next group, so Kaori and I left by another of the chapel's exits. I felt my heart vibrating. I looked at the people around me walking slowly or sitting down on the benches and praying silently, and they all looked pretty spaced out. We just sat down on the lawn near a garden and enjoyed the after-healing rush. Then

I noticed a bronze statue behind the bed of flowers across the square. Being very curious people, we got up and walked over to it.

It was a statue of the founder of the church, Frei Luis, and people were touching it and praying. Some wrote wishes or healing messages on small pieces of paper and placed them in the crannies between the statue's head and chest. Following their example, I wrote on a small piece of paper my wish that my mother, in Japan, would get healthier. I was placing it on the collar of the statue's neck when I heard a voice: "Hi, Japanese. What are you doing here?"

It was the English teacher, Alice, who had translated for Sérgio yesterday in front of Dr. Fritz's clinic. "What a surprise," I said. "What are you doing here?"

"I'm working here as a volunteer," she said. "I volunteer Monday and Tuesday at Dr. Fritz's hospital and here on Wednesday. Thursdays, Fridays, and Saturdays, I do my job as an English teacher." I thought to myself, "This woman is really dedicated!"

"That building over there is a hospital," Alice said. "It has eight different rooms. The first one is for kids and the eighth one is for seriously ill patients."

I asked, "Is it possible for us to go inside and see how they treat the patients?"

"No. It can't be done unless you are a disciple of Frei Luis," she said. "There are a quite a few spirit doctors here, too, who treat, heal, and cure patients. The doctors here don't use scalpels or scissors like Dr. Fritz, but they do remove tumors."

"What?" I exclaimed. "How can they do that without operating?"

"By the power of the spirits. A half hour ago I was at the side of a spirit doctor who put his hand on the abdomen of a patient and rubbed it. He didn't make any incision, but I saw a tumor come bubbling up from the skin. It doesn't always happen like that, but I see it every once in a while."

My intellect couldn't follow this. A tumor bubbling up from the skin was just too far out for me. So I asked her again and again, "Is this true? I don't believe it." But she said, "I swear to God. I never, never lie."

I had decided that during this trip to Brazil, unless I could see something clearly with my own eyes, I would put a mental question mark next to such phenomena. Even though Alice looked so honest and swore she was telling the truth, I never saw it with my own eyes, so I will just have to leave the reader in suspense.

You may be wondering what other Spiritist doctors have to say about the Dr. Fritz phenomenon. Dr. Paulo Cesar Fructuoso, a surgeon and Spiritist, speaks about this on the Dr. Fritz video: "I think that the tuning that happens between a spirit and a medium is programmed before we are born. The medium has a mission at a certain moment in his life when he meets the spirit, and from that moment on they perform charitable work together.

"Anyone can be a medium, independent of their belief, religion, intellectual level, sex, age, color, or race. Mediumship is inherent to the human species. All of us are mediums to a greater or lesser extent. All great mediums have most likely committed great sins in past lives. Arigó was a great medium and a great sinner in his past life. Edson Queiroz was the same, having committed errors in his past lives. I believe it's no different for Rubens. Mediumship is given to individuals as a form of paying back as quickly as possible their accumulated past debts."

Concerning reincarnation, Rubens himself explains, "One day, Dr. Fritz was a man, a being, and I believe he's come here to pay back for something he's done very wrong in the past. I've asked myself, 'Why me?' Fritz says that it's karma that I have to pay. Nowadays I don't ask anymore because he does such good things."

Before leaving, Kaori and I browsed through the book store, the chapel, and the grounds. Once again, I felt that spirituality was really alive in the country of Brazil.

On the way back to the hotel, we couldn't find a taxi, but an old lady in a wheelchair and her daughter managed to hail one, so we asked if we could squeeze in with them. Back at the hotel, we were so excited we couldn't stop talking about our new experiences. Kaori said, "We're so curious that tomorrow we're going to São Paulo! We're like Dr. Fritz groupies!"

We were in a very good mood and slept well.

THE MARATHON RUNNER WITH AIDS

November 28

São Paulo is a vast flat city with a population of 11 million and many high-rise buildings. It reminds me of Los Angeles, except that São Paulo has graffiti on nearly every wall and building.

While we were relaxing in our hotel room, Kaori pointed to the back of her neck and told me, "Maki-san, as I expected, the astral body injection from Dr. Fritz is working well. Go ahead and touch it." I touched the cervical vertebrae on the back of her neck and found that the swelling that had been there yesterday was completely gone. Her neck was smooth and healthy looking now.

"Wow, all the swelling is gone!" I said. "Congratulations! How about the pain?"

"I was wondering about that, too. I haven't felt any pain this morning. Did Dr. Fritz really cure it?"

I said, "Well, whoever did, I really hope you get healthier and happier." Then I asked, "So what are you going to have treated today?"

"For some time, I've been hearing an annoying sound in my ear, like a thump, thump, thump. If Dr. Fritz can cure that, it would be great."

"I don't know if he can cure it, but it can't hurt to try."

I never pushed Kaori to come to Brazil with the promise of a complete cure, but I was very glad that she was having a healing experience.

We were growing tired of eating our own simple Japanese food in our Rio hotel room, so we were both excited about the prospect of eating some good sushi in São Paulo's Japantown. But with our high expectations, we were very disappointed. The Japanese restaurant we found had a Santa Claus on the door dressed in a Japanese kimono. Over and over again a recorded voice repeated "*Irasshaimase*," which means "Welcome" in Japanese.

The meal we had was so disappointing that I don't even want to describe it here, but later, as we strolled around Japantown, we discovered that most of the Japanese-Brazilians were very kind. An older lady in a grocery store told us that Japanese-Brazilian taxi drivers were very reliable. We managed to find one and tried to locate Dr. Fritz's clinic. The driver, an older man, told us, "It's so much easier to speak Japanese than Portuguese." He spoke polite Japanese even better than a Japanese. I asked him why he had come to Brazil.

"I was born here," he said. "I've never been to Japan. But now São Paulo is becoming dangerous, and the cost of goods has nearly doubled. We used to have a lot of Japanese tourists, but nowadays you hardly find any." After driving for about a half hour, he said, "There are only factories around here. We're not going to find any hospital here."

"No, this is right," Kaori said. "Dr. Fritz's clinics are always located in this kind of area." Just then we saw someone in front of an old warehouse across the street trying to hail our taxi. Many street vendors were clustered around the gate. We had found Dr. Fritz's clinic.

Dr. Fritz used to treat patients five days a week in Rio de Janeiro and then come to São Paulo on Saturdays. Lately, however, he had changed his schedule so that he was in São Paulo on Thursdays and Fridays. I had heard that the owner of the crumbling warehouse had offered him the place for free because Dr. Fritz had cured his son of "incurable" lung cancer.

Dr. Fritz hadn't been treating people in São Paulo on Thursday for very long, so there were comparatively fewer patients at this clinic. Still, I counted at least 400. Everyone was sitting very quietly on chairs, and this clinic seemed a lot calmer and more composed than Rio de Janeiro's. The clinic room appeared to be on the second floor, so we started to climb up the stairs, but a broad-shouldered, middle-aged man blocked our way. This mighty sentinel wouldn't let anyone pass. I told him we were friends of Rubens and journalists from America, and finally he let us by. I noticed he spoke very clear, crisp English, and it occurred to me that he might act as a translator for us later.

When we got to the clinic room, we found about a hundred patients waiting there. Our timing was great. Rubens was just about to begin channeling Dr. Fritz, but we were able to say hello before he did. He welcomed us and said, "I can't believe you came all the way to São Paulo." Kaori said, "We're like rock star groupies. Wherever Dr. Fritz goes, we follow him." We all laughed, and Rubens asked, "Is there anything you want or need at this clinic?"

"It's more than enough of an honor just to watch you work and be in touch with your energy," I said. And I honestly meant it. Rubens sat down then and went through the same procedure to channel Dr. Fritz as he had in Rio de Janeiro.

Later, as I was busily snapping photographs of Dr. Fritz treating patients, a worker came over and cautioned me. I had permission from Rubens, so I didn't understand why this young man would not want us to take photos. "Sir, seven licensed doctors from renowned hospitals in the area are working as volunteers here today, and they really don't want the medical community to know they are here. It's okay to take photos, but please don't take any of the volunteer doctors." Now I realized that all the good-looking people in white clothing who were assisting Dr. Fritz were respectable medical professionals.

The injections continued for many hours. Dr. Fritz appeared more relaxed, as if he was enjoying himself more than at the Rio clinic. Perhaps it was because the patients were quieter and more orderly, or that there were fewer of them. Or maybe it was because so many doctors were eagerly helping him. I decided to go downstairs with my microcassette recorder and interview the man who had stopped us on the stairs.

"My name is Roberto," he told me. "I'm fifty-four years old. I used to work for Citibank and Ford Motor Corporation. That's why I speak English. Right now, I'm acting as a business consultant to six companies."

"Why do you volunteer here?" I asked.

"A half year ago I was diagnosed with terminal cancer of the colon. I wasn't in any pain, so the discovery was delayed until it was too late. No matter what hospital I went to, they told me it was too late to operate. Then I read about this clinic in a magazine. Dr. Fritz operated on me on the first day I came here. Later, at the regular hospital, they examined me and discovered that the cancer was totally cured. I really wanted to do something in return for Dr. Fritz, so I began volunteering here."

"How many hours a day do you work here? And do you get paid?" I asked.

"I'm working for free, of course," he said. "This morning I came at ten after six because patients start lining up that early. Sometimes I work until after one in the morning."

"What kind of religion do you believe in?" I asked.

"I try not to belong to any particular religious organization," he said, "But right now, my main interest is in Christianity and Spiritism, and I'm learning about Zen Buddhism."

When the interview was over, I thanked him, and he said, "I'm just one of many thousands of people who have been cured by Dr. Fritz. Let me find someone else who has been healed, and I can interpret for you." His zeal and eagerness surpassed my expectations.

A few minutes later, Roberto brought over a mother with a young boy on crutches. I could see that the child's leg was bent rather painfully. Roberto interpreted as the mother spoke: "My son's name is Rafael. He is seven. My name is Joseli. Rafael has suffered from polio for many years, but since we've been coming to Dr. Fritz for injections, he's gotten a lot better. Next week, Dr. Fritz is going to operate on his knees. The doctors at the hospital gave up a long time ago, saying it was impossible to operate. But Dr. Fritz told us that Rafael will be able to walk without crutches."

I asked her, "How did you find out about this clinic?"

"I heard about Dr. Fritz from my son. One day he was watching the news on television and Rubens was on the screen. All of a sudden, Rafael told me 'Mom, please take me to this person. This person is going to cure my leg.'"

"Wow," I said. "That's quite a story. So now Rafael is very happy?"

"Oh yes," she said. "He believes in Dr. Fritz from deep in his heart. Nowadays, I do too. I adopted my son, but because he had polio, I have been sad for many years. I thought of myself as an unlucky woman. Now I've changed my attitude. I'm very grateful and full of love. My son gave it back to me. Nowadays, every time I make cookies, Rafael says, 'Mom, it's okay with me if you just bring the cookies to Dr. Fritz to give away.'"

I thanked her for telling me her story, but she didn't want to end our conversation just yet. "Wait just a moment," she said, taking a photo from her wallet. "This is a photo of Rafael when he was a baby. If you want to put his pictures in your book, you can compare them with the photos of him today. Then you can use them as a message to people." As I looked at Rafael's leg in the photograph, I saw that it was short and thin and awkwardly bent inward.

Because we were in São Paulo, I thought there must be some Japanese-Brazilian patients there who could speak Japanese, so I began searching the waiting room. I found one family with a first-generation grandmother, a second-generation mother, and a third-generation son. The mother was wearing a Dr. Fritz T-shirt, and I was glad to learn she could speak a little Japanese. She said, "My name is Michiko Endo. This is my son, Eiichi. Grandma's name is Tsui."

"What brought you here?" I asked.

"I have a disease called alopecia areata, which causes my hair to fall out in circular patterns. But since I came here, it's gotten a lot better. The last week I was here, Dr. Fritz told me, 'You hair is growing very nicely.' And my body weight and cholesterol have also decreased dramatically."

I asked, "How about your grandmother and son?"

"Grandma has a disease in which stones accumulate in her abdomen, especially in her gall bladder. Next time, she is going to have an operation. My son has a disease called meningitis in his brain. His face used to be all drawn up, and he had cramps in his legs. He was suffering. But thanks to Dr. Fritz, now almost all the facial distortion is gone."

"So Dr. Fritz's treatments have been effective?"

"Oh yes. Dr. Fritz used to only come to São Paulo once a week, so once about 2,000 patients came at once."

"Are you getting treated with injections only?" I asked.

"Yes, but I know he is just pretending to give me injections, because I don't feel any pain at all. But you really have to believe in him from the heart. He told me many times that I have to pray for higher energy at nine in the morning and nine in the evening. I heard that Dr. Fritz is only expected to live four more years. He shares money with all the poor and elderly and gives away food to poor people. I think very highly of him. He is an amazingly compassionate person."

By the time I finished interviewing this simple homespun Japanese-Brazilian woman, Kaori came down from upstairs and said excitedly, "Maki-san, the operations are about to start." By the time I arrived in the operating room, Dr. Fritz had already finished operating on five patients, and he was just about to make an incision in the belly of a heavy, middle-aged Caucasian woman. This room was about three times larger and much cleaner than the one in Rio, but the biggest difference between Rio and here was the number of clever-looking doctors who were volunteering their help. As Dr. Fritz operated, he described to the six or seven doctors around him what he was doing .

Again, it was a very intense experience watching him operate. I could see five scissors and clamps protruding from the patient's belly, but still she was laughing and talking with the doctors, fully aware and conscious. As I observed the layers of fat and flesh revealed by the incision, suddenly I felt like crying. I said to myself, "I'm supposed to be used to these scenes, so why do I feel like crying again?" I tried to calm myself down, but my eyes became blurry with tears, and through them I felt I could see the care and love of all those doctors shining brightly.

Then Dr. Fritz extracted a red nugget of flesh from the woman's belly with a pair of tweezers. The operation apparently had been a success, because the doctors began applauding loudly. To me, it seemed like they were celebrating the victory of divine energy.

While other doctors stitched the patient up, Dr. Fritz, without a break, went right back to the clinic to inject another hundred patients.

I spied one of the doctors leaving. He had changed out of his white uniform into street clothes and was heading out the back door of the clinic. I chased after him, and near the parking lot I got a chance to interview him. Luckily, he spoke pretty good English.

"Please don't use my name. I'm thirty-four years old, and I've been practicing medicine for ten years. Three months ago, I began commuting here every week to study and be with Dr. Fritz."

"What kinds of things are you learning?" I asked.

"Many different things, but mainly quantum physics and quantum pharmacy. Dr. Fritz can manipulate the polarity of the membrane of the cerebral cortex with his universal energy. That's why there is no pain even without anesthesia. We are just beginning to learn the method to adapt that technique to our own hospital in a scientifically sound way."

"Could you explain more about this method?" I asked.

"At first, we are asked to train ourselves to raise our energy to a higher level. This is actually a practice of various kinds of meditation. One of the texts we are using right now is *Quantum Healing,* by Dr. Deepak Chopra."

"Have you scientifically examined any of Dr. Fritz's cases ?" I asked.

"Oh yes. The effectiveness of his treatments has been proven many times. For example, I had one patient with severe cancer. Dr. Fritz operated, and afterwards his symptoms dramatically improved. He was checked out using a computerized CAT scanner and MRI (magnetic resonance imaging), and it was proven that his cancer was totally cured."

"Are there any changes in your personal life since meeting Dr. Fritz?"

"Yes. My job, my family, my spiritual life: everything has changed in a big way. Most people are living in the material world focused on money, but I really hope those kind of people come here and learn the meaning of life and love and compassion."

In the video, Dr. Eleanor Luzes speaks about Dr. Fritz's teaching: "An important thing he has shown is his enormous interest in teaching doctors. So what does he say? It would be necessary for the doctors to develop their third-eye clairvoyance. This would be fundamental for diagnosis. This development would require of the doctors a correct diet and increased memory capacity. Beyond developing clairvoyance and memory, one must really reach the point of having control over magnetic fields, which appears to be something very difficult."

Dr. Paulo Cesar Fructuoso says, "Today we know that the medium has the capacity to see just with his own vision and diagnose internal tumors. So just imagine if a medical doctor could develop this capacity that's inherent in all of us. He wouldn't need a lot of sophisticated expensive equipment that is completely materially based, as is medicine today, which has very little spirituality. And besides being able to make diagnoses, he would know how to cure these diseases using his own energies, which exist in all of us."

Dr. Fritz explained in his own words: "You don't study this in the middle of the head. Study more here, between the eyebrows, the pineal gland. If you study here in the third eye, you will be able to do it. There's something here that helps, that hasn't been noticed. They say this is good for nothing. Ridiculous, it helps a lot."

After the interview with Dr. Marcello, I went to the bathroom. As I stood at the urinal, a skinny, pale young man came in. As soon as I saw him I thought he might be an AIDS patient. He spoke perfect English, with a New York accent. "I can speak English fluently, so I can interpret for you," he said. I thanked him for the offer but told him that Roberto was already interpreting for us and that I was more interested in hearing his story. He became rather excited and said, "Oh yes, of course. I would be glad to. My name is Carlos Anastácio. I'm thirty-five years old. It's been twelve years since I found out I had AIDS. The first year, I suffered a lot and thought I was going to die, but the second year, I began a macrobiotic brown rice and vegetarian diet, and began meditation and herbal treatments. With those treatments, I got better over the next ten years. Without the heavy symptoms of the disease, I survived. A year ago, all of a sudden, everything went wrong and I was hospitalized with hepatitis and colitis. I was operated on four times."

"How did you find out about Dr. Fritz?"

"Dr. Fritz is very very famous in Brazil. Even this morning, the Prudente newspaper had a big article about Dr. Fritz with three big photographs. Brazilians don't remember the name of the president, but they know the name of Dr. Fritz." He laughed faintly.

"So how many times have you been here?"

"I think today is my eighth time here. I'm not really sure. The first two times, I came in a wheelchair pushed by my father. I was in that bad a condition. When I saw Dr. Fritz the first time, I thought his energy was like that of Jesus Christ in a white doctor's uniform. He was emanating a bright light and showering those around him with it."

"Have you ever had an operation here?"

"No. I've only had injections of that magical brown liquid that narrow-minded scientists say is a poison."

"Since you started coming here, have your symptoms gotten better?"

"Oh yes, of course. Before I came I couldn't even go to the bathroom by myself. Now I have a lot more energy and a lot less pain. This morning, I went jogging with my dog for about thirty-five minutes. My goal at the moment is to participate in a full marathon, so that even after having AIDS for twelve years, I can run for forty-two miles to show the world the existence of spirit and the power of human will."

While I was interviewing him, his father came for him. I found out that his father was also being treated, for a backache. When their turn came, I was very curious to see how Dr. Fritz would use the syringe with an AIDS patient. I watched very carefully. After Dr. Fritz administered the injection, he threw it into a different bin from the one in which he had thrown hundreds of others. I heard that they were going to throw the syringes in the AIDS bin away. A question occurred to me. What if a latent HIV carrier came here and got injected? I read in the newspaper that in Brazil the epidemic of AIDS and HIV is severe; half a million people are said to be infected with HIV. Nowadays, even the Indios of the Amazon are rapidly getting infected. I didn't know if even Dr. Fritz could recognize an HIV carrier. I started to wonder whether we should be so optimistic about the sterilizing power of God.

It was eleven o'clock in the evening before Kaori could be treated. When her turn came, she said to Dr. Fritz, "I've been hearing annoying sounds in my ear, kind of a thump, thump. It won't go away." Dr. Fritz said, "Oh yes, I know that sound," and injected her behind her ear. More than fifty patients remained, so we decided to get back to the hotel.

As we left, Dr. Fritz was injecting a patient and waving to us at the same time.

THE PROPHECY OF KINKO SENSEI

November 29

I was becoming more and more interested in Brazil's rich history of spirituality, a spirituality that attracted and embraced the Dr. Fritz phenomenon. We decided that before going to the clinic, we would visit the Japan-Brazil Cultural Institute, near São Paulo's Japantown, to meet Koichi Mori, an anthropology professor. Professor Mori had long researched Japanese-related religions in São Paulo.

Brazil is a melting pot of many religions—Messianism, Kardecism, Santo Daime, União de Vegetal, Macumba (a catch-all category for Afro-Brazilian religions including Umbanda (a mixture of Candomblé, Kardecism, and Catholicism) and the black magic practices of Kimbanda)—far too many to describe here. Professor Mori told us, "The versatile race structure in Brazil has produced a spiritual-cultural mixture that is very rare in the world. To explain Brazilian syncretism briefly, I would say that the people in this country have not yet left the mythological realm. Most of the people feel the presence of God very closely in their daily lives, and they pray to animistic spirits and rely on psychic healing. This is a country where the gods and goddesses are still alive and active. Various Japanese religions have also been brought to the Brazilian people through the Japanese-Brazilians. Brazilians adopted these religions in their own way, mixing them with their other religions."

I once heard that the spirits who work with Dr. Fritz originally planned to carry out their medical activities in an English-speaking country. But when they researched the spiritual conditions on this planet, they decided to change their plans in favor of Brazil because so many people believed in the existence of spirits there. It was easier for them to be active in a country that believes in myths, and where the people are so poor and in need of healing.

A belief in the healing power of Catholic saints was introduced by the Church and continues today with the offering of wax body parts by those who are grateful to have received relief from their illness. Last time I was in Rio, I visited churches famous for being the destination of pilgrimages. The most interesting thing about these churches was not the main cathedral, but an attached room called "The Miracle Room." Inside this strange room, people had left so many wooden legs and arms and wax heads and hands that it looked like piles of broken mannequins.

Because our conversation with Professor Mori was so fascinating, it was four in the afternoon before we arrived at the clinic. At the entranceway, Roberto welcomed us and said, "Dr. Fritz has already treated the first 200 patients." I saw the exhaustion on his face.

"You look tired," I said. "Are you okay?"

"Last night Dr. Fritz treated 720 patients with injections and performed seventeen operations," he said. "When we finished, it was two in the morning. And today, the reason there are so many people waiting outside is that there is no space left in the waiting room." In a glance, I could see there were many more than the day before.

We went immediately to the operating room. Again today there were medical doctors gathered around the operating tables and helping Dr. Fritz. One of the patients was a middle-aged Japanese-Brazilian. When Dr. Fritz began working on him, he must have asked the man to count in Japanese, because he began reciting in a small voice: "*Ichi, ni, san, shi, go.*" While the man counted, Dr. Fritz incised his lower abdomen with a scalpel, leaving a bright red line that oozed a little blood. The operation took about five minutes. Then a volunteer doctor stitched up the man's incision. The patient then got up from the table, put on his T-shirt, and walked away all by himself. I chased after him to get an interview, catching up with him near the exit.

"Oh, I don't speak Japanese very well," he said "but my name is Mário Takara. I'm fifty-eight years old and a second-generation Japanese-Brazilian. I work in a car repair shop."

"What kind of operation did you have?" I asked.

"I don't know the exact word in Japanese, but there are stones in my urination tubes," he said. "It's hard for me to take a leak. It's been this way for two years, and it's been getting worse and worse."

"How long have you been coming to Dr. Fritz?"

"Today is the fifth time. I came for the first time about a month ago. My symptoms and disease have gotten a lot better."

"Did you get any anesthesia before Dr. Fritz operated on you?"

"No."

"When he cut your lower abdomen, did you feel pain?"

"I didn't feel much. I was afraid of it at first, though. But I'm really glad I got the operation."

"How much did Dr. Fritz charge you for the operation?" I asked.

"Oh no, no. He didn't charge me anything. That's why next time I come here I'm going to buy lots of cotton gauze to bring as a present to express my gratitude."

While I was interviewing Mr. Takara, I noticed a doctor standing nearby who had been assisting in the operating room. When I finished, he asked if I would interview him as well. He was the oldest of the volunteers, and it was obvious to me from the way everyone treated him that he was highly respected. He told me: "I am a specialist in anesthesia, and I used to work at the hospital in Santo André. My name is Dr. Geraldo Madeira. I just turned seventy."

I asked him, "Why did you begin working here as a volunteer?"

"I was seriously ill with cancer. The cancer in my pancreas had spread to other internal organs, so I gave up. I felt my time was very short. But a month ago, Dr. Fritz operated on me and I recovered. Yesterday, I got a detailed checkup using tomography, and it showed that all the cancer cells have disappeared."

"Tell me about your operation."

"I've been an anesthesiologist for more than thirty-five years, but I was operated on with no anesthesia whatsoever. I was fully conscious, and I was very, very surprised. There was absolutely no pain. Now I feel as though I have been reborn in my body and heart."

I thanked him for his time and went downstairs to the waiting room. Among the black and Caucasian faces, I saw quite a few Brazilian-Japanese faces. "Wow!" I thought happily, "Today's interviews are going to be easy." I was glad we had come all the way to São Paulo. I interviewed about a dozen people, but I will only share a few of the interviews here.

"My name is Sachiko Nagamine. I'm a second-generation Japanese-Brazilian, and I'm fifty-seven years old. I had so much pain in my legs that I couldn't sleep for months. Since I came to see Dr. Fritz two months ago, the pain has disappeared. Next week, he's going to operate on my leg, and I truly believe I'll be completely cured."

"My name is Yukie. I heard about this place from a close friend. She had terminal breast cancer, and her doctor gave her two months to live. She commuted here eleven times and tells me her cancer is perfectly healed. I also have cataracts. Dr. Fritz gave me an injection in my eye, but I didn't feel any pain at all. This is my seventh time here, and it's a lot better now. I can see much more clearly than before."

"My name is Emi Masaoka and I'm thirty-two. This baby is my son, Koji. He is eight months old. My son became blind because of a nurse's mistake in the premature baby unit. His eyes were burned by a laser beam. We've been here five times now. Little by little, my son's eyes seem to be getting better."

I felt a lot of warmth toward these simple and kind people. Because their parents and grandparents came from an older Japan, I sometimes felt they were more Japanese than the people now living in modern Japan. They seemed to have retained some of the old Japanese culture brought to Brazil generations ago.

As it got dark, the number of patients gradually decreased.

Dr. Fritz had been treating them at maximum speed. While he was injecting people in the clinic room, I went to visit the operating room for the third time. Eight patients were lying on beds waiting for surgery. At the bedside of one boy, who was to have an operation on his leg, the boy's father was deep in prayer. On the middle bed lay a young Chinese-Brazilian woman with her T-shirt tucked up so that her belly was exposed. I recognized her because she had been working as a volunteer nurse at Dr. Fritz's side the day before. On a corner bed lay a muscular young man who appeared cheerful and enthusiastic. A nurse was shaving the hair above his right ear. He didn't look sick, but I assumed that he was there for brain surgery. A few minutes later, Dr. Fritz came in, trailed by six or seven volunteer doctors. As usual, he immediately began making deft incisions in the patients. It was like watching a gardener with a very masterful technique for pruning tree branches. I watched him chisel into the young boy's leg, and in a moment the operation was over and the face of the boy's father flooded with relief.

The young Chinese nurse got an incision on her belly, and I became a little worried when she grimaced and winced as four pairs of scissors and two scalpels were inserted into the cut. But her twisted expression vanished in a few minutes, so I felt better. The rest of her surgery went smoothly. Then I witnessed something very surprising. Right after the young woman received stitches, she stood up, put on her white nurse's smock, gathered up the tools that had just been used to operate on her, and walked into an adjoining room. I followed her and watched as she washed the utensils and put them into a sterilizing liquid. Just five minutes ago, she had been operated on, and here she was working as a nurse already! It just blew my mind.

When I got back to the operating room, I saw that Dr. Fritz was about to do brain surgery on the cheerful young man. It seemed like the climax of the night's performance; the volunteer doctors were suddenly very interested and gathered closely around Dr. Fritz to watch him work. Dr. Fritz looked more serious now. He made a three-inch incision above the young man's ear, asked for a drill, and then drilled a hole in the patient's skull. The young man was fully conscious, and smiled at Kaori and me, who were standing next to his left leg. As Dr. Fritz drilled, the young man winked at us a couple of times, then joked with us by crinkling the corners of his eyes and rolling his eyes back into his head. I thought I had gotten used to such scenes, but I was amazed all over again. I had a notepad in my hand, so I began scribbling down my feelings. I wrote as though I was broadcasting live from the scene of the surgery. I am a little embarrassed now by the strong emotions I felt at the time, but I'll quote from my scribbled notes anyway:

An unbelievable thing just happened. Dr. Fritz stuck the pointed tips of a pair of scissors into the incision in the patient's skull and began hammering hard on the handle of the scissors with a metal stick held in his right hand. Although I felt like my own nervous system was writhing, I tried to keep looking into the face of this young man, and I saw his mouth and eyes were quite relaxed. His face showed no sign of going through something intense or of experiencing pain. I have heard that the brain is sort of numb, but Dr. Fritz was pushing the scissors into this young man's brain and tapping them like he was using a hammer and nail. I felt deeply moved, but instead of crying, I held my surprise and awe inside, feeling it go deeper and deeper until it touched my very core. My body began trembling, and I didn't think I could remain standing.

Then Dr. Fritz pulled out a long hypodermic needle and inserted it deep into the young man's brain. While he was pushing and wiggling the needle, he asked the young man to count in English. The man started counting quietly, "One, two, three," and I found myself listening intently and praying to God. The young man got to "four" and then said nothing for a little while. Then he continued, "seven, eight." I was startled and began worrying because he had skipped "five" and "six." All of a sudden, the doctors who were standing on the other side of the bed began praying for Dr. Fritz: "The grace of the Divine Light can heal the young and old. Praise for Dr. Fritz," and so on. Soon the others began extending the open palms of their hands toward the patient and praying also.

Then the young patient winked twice at the doctors and began counting again. This time he counted "One, two, three, four, five, six, seven, eight, nine, ten" without stopping. Everyone around him seemed to breathe easier, but continued praying. Then, at Dr. Fritz's request, the young patient raised his right leg, and then his left leg. The patient winked at me and Kaori again as we stood praying for him. Then suddenly he raised his right hand, and with his index and middle fingers, formed a peace sign. As he did so, Dr. Fritz removed the hypodermic needle and picked up a scalpel, pushing it deep into the brain and moving it up and down briskly.

Then, all of a sudden, Dr. Fritz said something in a loud voice, and everyone burst into laughter. The laughter seemed to be over-flowing with love. All the doctors' eyes were glowing, and I felt the entire operating room suddenly brighten up. The doctor standing next to me whispered in my ear, "The operation was a great success. He cleaned out all the cancer cells." Then I really felt I had seen the work of divine energy.

The other patients, who were waiting their turn in the operating room, began hugging the doctors and nurses, expressing their joy over the success of the young man's surgery. Dr. Fritz, however, didn't seem flattered or drunk with the ecstasy of success, but moved immediately to the next patient, a middle-aged Caucasian woman, and made an incision on her back.

Kaori and I were far too inspired to move from the bedside of the young man. On his head, I could see the incision and a little blood. Then a doctor began stitching up the incision, and the young man looked at Kaori. I followed his eyes and noticed that Kaori had on a waist pouch, and that the zipper on the pouch was halfway open. The young man reached out and closed the zipper for her, saying, "Be careful. You're going to get robbed." While he was getting stitches! I really don't like to use the word 'miracle' very often, but right now I really want to use it. This *is* a miracle.

About ten minutes later, a nurse put some gauze on the wound and the young man stood up next to his bed and gave

Kaori and I a big hug. He flashed us the peace sign again, and we took some photos together. While this was going on, I said, "A lot of people don't believe such things can happen. They are very skeptical and think things like this are just setups, so I might have to come back again to do more research. If you have a business card, could you give it to me?" He patted his pockets, then said, "Oh, I have a card in my car in the garage. I'll get it for you right away." Then he *ran* full tilt to the parking lot! Kaori and I turned to look at each other's astonished faces. We were speechless.

He ran back with his business card in hand and gave it to us. We stood watching as he got back into his car and drove away.

Later on, as Dr. Fritz continued to treat others, we wished him good-bye and told him we would see him again in Rio de Janeiro. Then we returned to our hotel.

November 30

Our return flight to Rio didn't leave until that evening, so we decided to visit a Shinto priestess in São Paulo named Kinko Sensei. Sensei means "teacher" in Japanese. I had read about her in some Japanese anthropology books. Also, Professor Mori at the Japan-Brazil Cultural Center had told us about her. He said she was an open-hearted, frank person. He was sure we would be able to meet her.

When we hailed a taxi from Japantown, the one that stopped for us was driven by the same Japanese-Brazilian driver we had met before. I thought, "Wow, great timing again." After driving half an hour through São Paulo, he dropped us off at a small park. According to the address we had been given, it was the right place. But Kinko Sensei was the priest of a Japanese Shinto shrine, and we didn't see any buildings that looked like a shrine anywhere in the park's vicinity. We checked the address again, but we were almost positive it was correct. The only thing we could find was a shady-looking liquor store with an old alcoholic-looking man inside who was drinking a shot of liquor.

All of a sudden, Kaori yelled, "Maki-san! I found it. Look over there!" She pointed to a spot above the liquor store, and I saw the toy-like red symbol, called a *torii*, which means "gateway to the entrance of a Shinto shrine." The little torii was attached to a white wall above the liquor store, so we went inside and asked after Kinko Sensei. A few moments later she came down to greet us. She wore an old sweater and spoke in an authentic and lively Osaka dialect. "I'm glad to see you folks. You came all the way from Japan, didn't you?"

We explained that we lived in the United States, and she led us across the street to her home, which housed the Shinto shrine. As we crossed the road, a Japanese girl, who looked to be about five years old, ran toward us and shouted "*Bom dia!*" Kinko Sensei scolded, "You don't say '*bom dia*' to Japanese people. You say '*konnichiwa.*'" Then the little girl said, "*Konnichiwa!*" and ran off into the liquor store. Kinko Sensei told us this child was the fourth-generation successor to the Shinto shrine. "She is my granddaughter," she said. "She has even stronger psychic ability than her mother, and can do the esoteric spiritual ceremony all by herself."

Kinko Sensei led us inside her house, which had red wooden walls. In the rear, a huge room served as the shrine. "You don't need to use the honorable preface *sensei* with me," she told us, "Everybody calls me Dona Kin-chan, all right?" (*Chan* is the Japanese diminutive ending.)

I was beginning to see why people described her as natural and frank, but as we listened to the story of her life, I began to think she was far beyond any psychic priest I had ever met before. She was very eloquent, and her story was moving and inspiring. She told us about her mother, the founding priest of the shrine, and about the spiritual climate of Brazil.

In the Japanese book *Research on Japanese Religion and Japanese Brazilian Religion,* by Dr. Hiromichi Nakamatsu, Kinko Sensei was introduced in this way: "In 1983, the northeastern part of Brazil was attacked by a severe drought for six consecutive years. At that time, the spirit of a Catholic priest, Padre Cícero, appeared to Kinko Sensei. Saint Cícero was no longer alive, having died fifty years before, but he was still famous, and well respected as a saint who could perform miracles. Saint Cícero asked Kinko Sensei to pray to the Japanese Shinto gods for rain. When she did so, the Shinto gods sent this message through her: 'In 1984, the Dragon Goddess promises to pour lots of rain over the northeastern part of Brazil.' The record shows that a big rain came and alleviated the drought."

Kinko Sensei told us, "When I get a message from the Divine Word, I don't think anything in my head. My brain is just empty, and my mouth just moves spontaneously, without my intending it to. If you would like to ask the gods some questions, I can give it a try for you."

The truth was, we had been waiting for her to offer! I said, "Kinko Sensei, could you ask the Japanese Shinto gods what precautions I should take for the rest of my life?" She straightened her spine and her face took on a mystical expression. Then she picked up a book of Shinto scripture from the desktop and banged it loudly on the desk several times. Finally, in an incredibly loud voice, she said, "You are going to travel a lot, so please be careful not to lose your luggage, especially your camera. But if something happens, then the Goddess of the Substitute will come to your aid. So don't worry."

I asked my second question: "I'm publishing books, comic books, and a music CD both in the United States and Japan. Which country should I emphasize with my marketing?" She banged the books loudly on the desk again and said, "In Japan, they have the goodness of the Japanese. In the United States, they have the goodness of Americans. So why restrict your marketing to these two countries? You can expand your market to the entire world! You can fly over the entire planet! Be more ambitious! Hii-ya!" She delivered these communiqués with incredible vigor.

I said, "Oh yes, yes! That's a great message!" When she returned from her short trance, Kinko Sensei said, "That was the male god, named Gonnodaiyu Inari Daimyojin. This god is always very clear and speaks in black and white terms with a lot of power."

"Thank you so much," I said. "Here is my last question: I have read and heard about many channelers predicting many changes to occur around the year 2000 on this planet. What is the perspective of the gods and goddesses of the Japanese Shinto shrine on this?" She banged the divine book again, making even bigger sounds, and seemed to go into an even deeper trance. It was awesome to watch. Her mouth began moving, and then she gave us this divine message: "Seichi Inari Daimyojin, the main god, says something will certainly happen, but we can't announce it publicly because it will cause a panic. Similar things have happened in planetary history, but on a smaller scale."

Suddenly, this voice was interrupted by the voice of Gonnodaiyu Inari Daimyojin, the god we had heard earlier: "As gods, why don't we openly announce to human beings where and what kinds of things are going to happen?"

But the voice of Seichi Inari Daimyojin returned and said, "If you announce the prophecy outright, a lot of people will get nervous and panic. When it happens, we will try to save as many people as we can."

As Kinko Sensei came out of her trance, she told us that Gonnodaiyu Inari Daimyojin had predicted the merging of East and West Germany and the war between England and Argentina over the Falkland Islands long before they actually happened. "But if they say when and where this big catastrophe is going to happen, then it will be like people are living in hell. They won't be able to feel alive and happy knowing that such a big thing will happen in a few years."

As we wished her good-bye, she said, "For the sake of Brazilian friendship, please write good things about Brazil and the Brazilian people."

Her powerful energy was contagious, and all the way back to the hotel we were kind of high from the experience. When we got back, I concentrated on writing Christmas cards to my friends while sitting at a nice desk in the hotel lobby. I had bought forty cards that morning and was eagerly immersed in the task. I took off the fishing vest I was wearing and laid it on the chair in front of me. This vest has eight pockets, which fit my camera and film perfectly, so I always keep them in there. About halfway through the stack of cards, I laid down my pencil and looked over at the chair. I panicked. My vest and camera had disappeared! Suddenly the Shinto god's message came to mind: "Be careful with your camera." As I sat there feeling lost and disappointed, Kaori came in from outside. I rushed over to her. "Did you take my fishing vest?" I asked.

"No! What happened? Don't you always put your camera in the pocket of that vest?"

"Gosh," I said. "My best camera, the professional titanium one, was just stolen right from this chair."

"Weren't you just warned about this by Kinko Sensei? You have to be more careful!"

"Wow," I said. "I didn't think the prediction would manifest this quickly. I can't believe it. I can replace the camera, but the film I shot can't be replaced. There are a lot of good photos of Dr. Fritz's operations in the camera."

I couldn't do anything about it other than to report it to the front desk. Afterwards, I went back to writing Christmas cards to take my mind off my loss. Kaori decided to write her Christmas cards too, and opened up her shoulder bag. All of a sudden, she exclaimed, "Ah, I found it, Maki-san! Your camera and film are in my bag. But how did they get in here?"

I literally jumped for joy. Then I remembered the Shinto God's message through Kinko Sensei: "You have to be especially careful about your camera. But if something happens, the Goddess of the Substitute is going to help you out, so don't worry!"

In my heart I said, "Thank you so much, Goddess of the Substitute. You have saved my camera and film."

A SECRET SEALED
IN A STATELY MANSION

December 1

Early in the morning, we dressed up very nicely because we had been invited to attend a Sunday party at the stately mansion of Cesarina Riso, a famous high-society figure in Rio de Janeiro. Four days before, as we stood waiting to see Dr. Fritz in his clinic room, I had noticed a noble-looking middle-aged woman standing next to us. With one glance, I could tell she was wealthy.

After making eye contact several times, she spoke to me quietly in beautiful English, thereby confirming her status. She said her name was Cesarina Riso, and that she had inherited a huge, historic rubber plantation from her parents. She was the wealthy daughter of a rich family.

She told me that Dr. Fritz had cured her of several diseases. "It's quicker to get treatment here than at the big hospital," she said. "Besides, Dr. Fritz's cures work better." She told me that every Sunday afternoon she had a party for the Who's Who of Rio de Janeiro: writers, musicians, politicians, and people associated with the movies. When she discovered I had published several books in Japan, she invited Kaori and me to her mansion.

If you mention high-class areas in Rio, most outsiders picture fashionable Ipanema Beach. But for locals, the more exclusive area is São Conrado Beach, right next to Ipanema. Cesarina's mansion is situated on a hill at São Conrado, overlooking the ocean. When we arrived, two gatekeepers in smart uniforms opened the gate for us, and from there it took more than a few minutes, passing through huge rain forest-like gardens, to drive to the house on top of the hill. It was a colonial-style mansion, surrounded by uncountable exotic tropical flowers. It nearly took my breath away. When I saw the artistic private chapel, large enough for a few dozen people to pray together, the words, "high society" took on a new meaning for me.

A servant in a pure white colonial uniform escorted us into the main house. It seemed more of an art museum than a living space. In the large hall, a pianist and bassist were playing light, soothing Bossa Nova music. A steaming buffet table was crowded with a few dozen exotic Brazilian dishes, all of which made our mouths water. Taking in all the polite well-trained servants and beautifully dressed guests while listening to the music, I felt like I had wandered onto the set of an epic movie—*Gone with the Wind*, perhaps. I marveled at the person who could host such a gorgeous elaborate party every Sunday and wondered about the disparity of wealth between these guests and Kaori and I, who were cooking rice in our hotel bathroom.

Then our hostess came to welcome us, wearing a fancy dress. She was far more impressive in these surroundings than at the clinic where we had met. She looked quite grand and very digni-fied as she led us to a large table and introduced us to several renowned playwrights. As Kaori and I became absorbed in sam-pling the exotic cuisine, I spied David Sonnenschein among a group of newly arriving guests. I waved at him, and when he saw us, he and his wife came to our table wearing big smiles and a look of surprise. "Welcome back to Rio!" David said enthusiastically. "I didn't know you guys were invited to this party."

I said, "That's my favorite line! I didn't expect to meet you here." The Sonnenscheins had invited us to come to their house the day after next. I introduced Kaori to them.

"How do you do?" David asked. "I know a lot about you from reading the English edition of Maki's book *Spiritual Adventures of a Sushi Chef*. This is my wife, Anna."

Kaori explained how we came to be invited to Cesarina's party. David told us that Cesarina was an avid supporter of his movie,

Arigó and Dr. Fritz. As we ate, David told us the names and ingredients of each of the Brazilian dishes, but I was more interested in talking about Dr. Fritz. I had tons of questions in my head, and I couldn't wait until the visit to his house. "David," I said, "I feel like it isn't just a coincidence that we were both invited here today. I think it's a great opportunity. Would you mind talking with me about the Dr. Fritz phenomenon today?"

David spoke with his wife in Portuguese for a few minutes and then said, "Okay, that would be fine. I'm sorry I've been too busy to help with your research this time. My wife has to do something with our children, so she needs to go back home. But let's find a quiet place to talk." After wishing his wife good-bye, we found a perfect spot on a courtyard bench surrounded by beautiful trees, flowers, and singing birds. I was glad that I had brought my microcassette recorder with me. I clipped the little microphone to David's shirt pocket and began the interview.

"First, could you tell me about your plans for your next motion picture?"

"I'm planning to make a big-screen movie of the life of Arigó, who was the first medium to channel the spirit of Dr. Fritz. His life story is so touching and inspirational. I've finished the script already, and now I'm gathering investors and selecting the actors and actresses. I'm planning to cast internationally known talent for the major roles and have spent some time already with Academy Award-winning actor Jon Voight, who expressed a great interest in the movie when we met in Manaus."

I had just seen the Tom Cruise movie *Mission Impossible*, in which John Voight played the role of the chief of the spy unit. Actually, when I was at the Tropical Hotel in Manaus, I saw him nearly every day on the walkway or restaurant, because he was there with a film crew shooting *Anaconda* on location in the Amazon jungle. John seemed like a New Age person to me, because he spoke at the opening ceremony of the ITA conference about environmental issues, especially the devastation of the rain forest.

"Do you view Rubens and Dr. Fritz as two different personalities in one physical body?"

"Oh no, not at all," he said. "I have been communicating with Rubens and Dr. Fritz as totally different individuals. I see them as absolutely different people. They have different knowledge, different personalities, different desires, different strengths and weaknesses."

"Could you describe the characteristics of the two?"

"Rubens is a typical Brazilian. He likes to party. He's charismatic, likable, friendly, cultured, and international. He likes to play with electronic toys and gadgets. He really likes women a lot. Actually, Rita is his third wife."

"Does his adopted daughter live with him?"

"His daughter is six years old and visits him only on weekends. Rubens is kind of a normal guy who usually doesn't like to say no. But Dr. Fritz is totally different. He is extremely focused. One thing he says about the difference between incorporating and incarnating: When you are in your own body, born into this lifetime, you have free will. But when you are a spirit incorporated into some medium, you don't have free will. Fritz has a mission, and he can't escape that mission. His actions and words are extremely consistent. There is a lot of ambiguity and all that, but the presentation and purpose of the mission is singular and unwavering. For example, for all these years Rubens has had to decide what to do with his business, his kids, and his personal life—back and forth and this and that. But Fritz has been consistently focused on his mission. Fritz has a lighter side and can laugh, but he also has a—what's the word?—stern and forceful side. When people don't behave how he wants them to, he gets intense and verbally aggressive toward them. Of course he has to deal with a thousand patients every day, so he needs to be straightforward."

"Do Rubens and Dr. Fritz have a mutual memory, one they share?"

"Yes. I think Fritz is conscious of Rubens' experience, but not so much the other way round. Sometimes, however, Fritz definitely doesn't remember Rubens' experience. For example, once my friend Alemão drove Rubens eight hours to São Paulo. When they got there, Rubens incorporated Dr. Fritz and started to work on the patients. Then he looked at Alemão and said, 'Oh, you're here!' Again, this may be because Fritz isn't just one thing. It is not a single phenomenon explained by a singular linear experience. Sometimes it crosses over. There is not one explanation to give you a total map of the experience, you know. Rubens usually doesn't remember what happened when he was incorporated with Dr. Fritz's spirit."

"I've watched Rubens work for hours without a break. Doesn't he get tired?"

"It depends on the day. He has two different kinds of reactions to this kind of work. One is that Rubens is unconscious while working all day and when he comes back he is ready to start his day and his wife is very tired, but he wants to go out to eat or party or whatever. So, during the work, no time passes at all for him."

"He doesn't remember?"

"No, not at all. On the other hand, sometimes when he comes back from Fritz, he is totally exhausted. He can't even stay awake and just needs to get back home and go to bed. So he lives both versions, depending on the day."

"Does Dr. Fritz take good care of Rubens' physical health? How does he do it?"

"I don't think Rubens can be perfectly managed for optimum health. He looks healthy, but actually sometimes he is not feeling well. Once I saw Dr. Fritz help Rubens with his heart problem, but other times when Dr. Fritz is working I've seen that Rubens' doesn't feel very well, and he asks his nurse to check his blood pressure. When he is working too long, his blood pressure gets too high and he has to take some prescription drugs to lower it. So that means that Dr. Fritz can't hold Rubens' total physical condition."

"How many mediums have been channelers of Dr. Fritz?"

"There are more than a dozen so-called self-proclaimed Dr. Fritzes in Brazil. Right now, there are five or six Dr. Fritzes treating patients. But through Rubens, Dr. Fritz has acknowledged only four mediums in the authentic lineage. The first was Zé Arigó, then Oscar Wilde, then Edvaldo, and the last was Edson Queiroz."

"How does he distinguish between authentic and fake?"

"Rubens has said that you can find out if it is really Dr. Fritz or not with three tests," David said. "One is whether he speaks German. When Rubens is incorporated with Dr. Fritz, he is able to speak German. Sometimes it seems to me that he understands German even better than Portuguese or English. Several people have asked him a question that he didn't quite understand, but through a German interpreter, he understood completely."

Actually, I've heard Dr. Fritz speak in German more than a few times, but the only words I could understand were the numbers "*einz, zwei, drei.*"

"The first medium, Arigó, spoke German, right?," I asked.

"Yes. Arigó was a young, uneducated farmer, but when he incorporated with Dr. Fritz, he spoke fluent German. So that's one of the tests he described. The second is that Dr. Fritz has vast knowledge in many areas of science: medicine, biology, chemistry, physics—particularly in quantum physics."

"Quantum physics wasn't discovered till after World War I, right?"

"Yes, that's correct. That's another logical loop we have to figure out. Did his life stop when he died, or did his intellect stop when he died? Apparently that doesn't apply to this Dr. Fritz phenomenon. Even from the Kardecist point of view, if a person dies, the spirit has been active all these years. He has access to new information. So it's not like the dead are dead and don't evolve anymore. But many people have that question, because they think it can't be. How could he do this?

"These are the first two guidelines. But honestly, these first two don't guarantee the authenticity of Dr. Fritz, because I could speak German and have a vast knowledge of science. So if you have those two qualities, it still doesn't guarantee that the person is authentic. But the third one is more interesting. Dr. Fritz said he is able to recognize people from his previous incorporation with other mediums. In other words, when Dr. Fritz was working with Arigó, Arigó treated patients, and now when Rubens is incorporated with Dr. Fritz, he recognizes the same patients—not only recognizes them, but can identify particular elements, like the person's disease. I've seen that happen—Dr. Fritz's response to a person he has seen through a previous medium. He's very personal and makes comments about that person and their relationship to the previous medium and what happened during that period. Dr. Fritz even calls them by the nicknames they used to use in that period. So to me that would be the most interesting thing to authenticate Dr. Fritz."

"According to my research," I said, "the previous Dr. Fritz, Edson Queiroz, died in 1991, and Rubens started to channel Dr. Fritz in 1983. That means they were staggered, that Dr. Fritz was appearing in two different people at the same time."

"I asked Dr. Fritz about this at one time," David said, "and he told me it's not necessary to manifest through a single person at one time, because the Dr. Fritz phenomenon transcends time and space. This is another issue he talks about that is very fascinating. His time is not the same as ours. He doesn't use the clock. He measures time by magnetic waves. Literally, it's in the area of quantum physics. He says that time is the folding of the magnetic wave, which is something beyond my understanding. He uses these magnetic waves not in theory but in the practical healing field, specifically healing the incisions he has opened. For example, the bones he drills in brain surgery, these close almost immediately."

"So it's bone rejuvenation?"

"Yes. It's also called bone regeneration. He describes it partly as 'putting it back in time.' He has the ability to use magnetic fields to reverse time—in other words, to put the tissues back into another time and space when they were healthy and normal. This is, to me, an extremely fascinating idea. But again, he is actually using this to cure the patients."

"I heard that the spirit of Dr. Fritz is not alone, that there are a number of spirits with him. Is that right?"

"That's another issue. Dr. Fritz is like a spokesman, the verbal part of a lot of other spirits and entities."

"So how many are there?"

"He has over three thousand there to support his treatment.

There is a level of different specialist for each medical problem—gynecologist, orthopedist, dermatologist. All the different specialists work on specific cases."

"Do the other doctors have a name like Dr. Fritz?"

"There is one in particular. His name is Dr. Ricardo, who apparently has incorporated with another medium as well. He sometimes takes over Rubens' body without saying anything. He deals with deeper surgery. He's a specialist in opening up peoples' bodies. He likes to open them up. Sometimes he makes large incisions that are unnecessary."

David told us a few stories about this Dr. Ricardo that made Kaori and I uneasy. We began to laugh nervously, but David was pretty serious about it, so we settled down. "I saw one operation," David continued, "where he opened the belly of one patient about three or four inches and then stuck in tiny needles. Maybe he was doing some energy work or something, but I was thinking, 'Those tiny needles could fit in a much smaller incision.'"

"So that means that Dr. Ricardo took over Rubens that time?" I asked.

"Yes, most likely. Another aspect of Dr. Ricardo is that he doesn't talk much. Once while I was interviewing Dr. Fritz for the movie script about the life of Arigó, several questions came up, so I asked Dr. Fritz, 'Is it possible for me to talk to the spirit of Arigó?' He said, 'Oh, yeah.' So I said, 'Really? How can I do that?' He said, 'Just tell me when you want to and I'll call him.'

"So the next day I went back with a list of questions. When I got there, Dr. Fritz was about to operate on a woman lying on the bed. I asked him if I could talk to Arigó, and he said 'Okay, I'll call him.' He sat down on the chair and went into a trance for about twenty seconds. When he came out of the trance, he opened his eyes and looked around and didn't say anything, but he grabbed the surgical tools off the table and picked up a kind of serrated wire, like a saw. He took it over to the woman, put it under her chin, and began sawing back and forth on her neck.

"There were a few people watching this scene, wondering what was going on. The woman was making a noise like 'aagghhh,

aagghhh,' and people began touching my shoulder, saying, 'Go on, talk to him. Talk to him.' So I said, 'Hello, who is there?' He said in a low voice, 'Dr. Ricardo.' He didn't speak at all after that.

"After he finished the operation he sat down on the chair, and after a short trance, Rubens came back. It was funny that Rubens didn't know what was going on. After that Rubens channeled Dr. Fritz and he said, 'Well, did you get to talk with Arigó?' So it was obvious that there was no communication between those spirits."

"Gosh, that's too much," I said.

"Yes, it was a truly remarkable incident. But about the multiple spirits—Dr. Fritz says that each patient who is treated at the clinic has an individual spirit accompanying him, so that when Dr. Fritz treats the patient, he spends ten seconds with each. It's not because he's figuring out in ten seconds what is wrong with the patient, but rather that the patient has already had a complete diagnosis by another entity who specializes in that particular area, and that entity guides Dr. Fritz on how to treat the patient."

"I've heard that before. Now it's beginning to make sense to me," I said.

"That's one of the interpretations about how work goes on in this invisible world," David said. "Also, that the spirit continues to accompany the patient through the healing process afterwards."

As we were talking, Rubens' wife came up to us and said hello. She and David conversed for a few minutes in Portuguese. Then she returned to the main house, where the party was still in progress. David told me that Rita and Rubens were invited to the party, but that Rubens was not feeling well, so he was at home in bed all day. "Maybe he caught a cold or was too exhausted," David said. "It's too bad, eh?"

I didn't know what to say. Maybe that was how karma worked, but I felt very sorry for Rubens and his wife.

We continued. "Can you define the Dr. Fritz phenomenon in a few words?"

"It's impossible in a few words. I think he is a paradigm destroyer. He doesn't fit into a single interpretation. That's why I like this so much. You can pursue it from the scientific side, the psychological side, the energy side, or Spiritist side. All these different paradigms can be applied, but none of them can completely explain what's going on. My work as a filmmaker is to get people to open their eyes to all these things. It's a kind of holographic view of the world, in which lots of things are reflected but not any one is all-encompassing."

"I heard that Dr. Fritz is teaching professors and doctors about his technology."

"Yes, sometimes he gives a series of lectures to intellectuals, as well as the general public. But there are some difficult aspects to that because in his world, science has progressed overwhelmingly. So regular scholars, scientists, and doctors can't really understand his teachings, and they are having difficulty adapting it to their own terminologies, because most of these things are going on in the invisible world. It's like teaching a baby who can't even stand yet to ride a bicycle. So first we need to train the baby how to stand up and walk."

"I heard someone say that the spirit group working with Dr. Fritz is a group of extraterrestrials. What do you think?"

"That depends on what you consider the ET phenomenon to be, whether you use the word extraterrestrial as a psychological symbol, see it as an energy phenomenon, or recognize it as a physical being, like a spaceman. If you would like to do further research into this issue, I recommend you meet Dr. Gilda Moura. She is a psychologist who has been researching the Dr. Fritz phenomenon, as well as the brain waves of UFO abductees."

"I know Dr. Moura!" I said. "She was a speaker and presenter at the ITA conference in Manaus, right? I went to her workshop. She was on your Dr. Fritz video, wasn't she?"

"Yes, that's right. So you know about her. Tomorrow evening I'm invited to attend her lecture and book signing at the planetarium."

"That's good timing," I said. "I'll go too."

"She's giving the lecture in Portuguese, but at least you can meet her. Perhaps then you might be able to get an appointment to interview her."

"Yes, thank you so much. Now for my last question. What do

you think about the mission of Dr. Fritz's spirit group on this planet? He keeps saying that he is trying to heal the human spirit through healing the human body...."

"That's correct. His mission uses disease and the body. He is trying to heighten the levels of human consciousness and spirituality. He would like to show people that there is a wonderful world that is invisible beside the material world. He likes people to believe in themselves and God. His ultimate message is that we are all connected to one other, that we and nature and the universe are ultimately one. Oneness is the truth."

"That's pretty similar to New Age philosophy." I said.

"Yes, that's why part of his therapeutic method for heart awakening is to have patients wait in line for ten hours for their turn. Those patients perceive the pain and suffering of the other patients around them, and through that experience they can connect to each other and feel empathy and compassion for each other. So pain can be the tool to gain unconditional love and deep awakening. And when Dr. Fritz takes the pain away in a miraculous shocking way, then there's an opportunity to raise up the human spirit and spirituality. He said, 'If I can heal the spirits of ten people out of one thousand patients, that is a big success, because those ten people can heal another hundred people in their communities.' So that means Dr. Fritz is not just catching fish and delivering them to people. He is actually teaching how to fish and seeding the spirit of love."

"That's very inspiring. So your video and the film about Arigó is also one of those projects to seed the spirit of love?"

"Yes, I believe so. I'd like to deliver Dr. Fritz's message to more than the thousand patients who come to the clinic every day. I would expect that of the book you are writing."

"Oh, I don't know what I can do, because I'm not that famous.... Besides, I don't want to write a book that just advertises and praises Dr. Fritz. But I think I'll be happy if I can describe the phenomenon exactly as I saw it with my eyes and heard it with my ears, without exaggeration."

"That's a very appropriate attitude toward your writing. Me

too. In my video, I'm not blindly hero-worshipping Dr. Fritz. So, is that all of your questions?"

"Well, I thought of one more thing I wanted to ask. Is that okay?"

"Sure. I'm taking the bus home anyway, so I still have a little time until then."

"My gut feeling is that the spirit group working with Dr. Fritz didn't just come into this world during World War I. I think they've been here a long time, maybe even a few thousand years. What do you think?"

"Actually, you are right."

"I'm very curious about that point. I'd love to hear a more detailed explanation."

"Uh... yes," he murmured. Until that moment, David had been very eloquent and talkative. All of a sudden, he began mumbling, and seemed reluctant to open his mouth. "I wish I was in a position to tell you everything I know," he said finally. "Dr. Fritz has given me some amazing messages during my interviews. His messages were more astonishing than any of his miraculous surgeries. Channelers of New Age books say similar things, but they only speak about what they've heard from outer space or whatever. Dr. Fritz, however, is actually using the knowledge from that world and proving it big-time with his abilities to heal people. In fact, because he has actually treated 350,000 patients, and their recovery is so solid, I have to think that whatever he says I must accept as truth."

"What are you trying to tell me exactly? You're giving me a very long prelude...."

"What I'm trying to say is that I was told not to publicly report the incredibly long history of this spirit group, or their even more amazing knowledge and techniques and stuff."

"Who told you this?"

"Dr. Fritz, of course. I've already done interviews, recorded, and filmed these things, but I didn't put this stuff into my video because I was told the time is not yet right to announce these secrets to the public."

"What do you mean by that?" I asked, my interest growing.

"Because it goes too far beyond our common sense, so people can't effortlessly accept and understand it. People might be too shocked. As I said, similar things have already been announced through several channeled New Age books, but at the moment Dr. Fritz would like to keep his work inside the framework of being the spirit of Dr. Fritz."

"So if I don't announce it publicly, is it okay for you to tell me?"

"That's right."

"So this will be strictly between you and us. I'm not going to write it down in my book. Now can you tell us?"

"You definitely won't write about this?"

"I promise. Please believe me."

"If you promise that, I can tell you. But before I do, would you turn off the cassette recorder?"

"No problem," I said, and I turned it off. Then, for the next ten minutes, Kaori and I sounded like this:

"Oh really?"

"Wow!"

"Whew!"

As a writer of non-fiction, I thought, "What a waste not to be able to write this down!" But I don't want to break my promise to David and Dr. Fritz. If I do, it might affect my karma. So I'm going to suppress the desire of my hand—and the pen that trembles in it—from writing about what I heard. I will try to persuade my hand that the readers of this book might even enjoy knowing that there are some secrets I will never be able to reveal.

I was more than satisfied with my unplanned interview. When we got back to the main house, the gorgeous party was over, so the three of us thanked Cesarina for inviting us and began walking down the long garden road toward the gate. About halfway down, we saw a car coming toward us with a baby in the back seat. Anna, David's wife, was driving it. "I finished my business with the kids early," she said, "so I came here to check on you. But I didn't expect you to still be here."

Again, it was good timing for us. David and Anna gave us a

ride to our hotel. Back in the hotel room, Kaori said, "But Maki-san, the annoying sounds in my ears haven't gone away yet. Let's go see Dr. Fritz tomorrow for one last treatment."

"Okay, Kaori-san, but I don't want to miss meeting Dr. Moura at the planetarium in the evening. So we need to be at the clinic very early in the morning to get a number that's at least under 100."

"All right," she said. "That means I'll just have to wake up at five o'clock tomorrow morning!"

Hearing her determination, I thought, "She's even more into Dr. Fritz than I am!"

The DNA Cord
Between Mother and Child

December 2

Kaori did her best. She must have woken at five, because around six, her cheerful voice reached my sleepy ears: "Wake up Maki-san. The rice and miso soup are ready."

After eating our simple breakfast, we hopped into a taxi. Once again, we got caught in heavy traffic, so it was already almost eight o'clock when we arrived. When we got out at the gate, my heart sank as I saw the long long line with no end in sight. Kaori and I followed it back, turning two corners before we finally found the end, and took our places.

"So much for our strategy to be among the first hundred people here," I complained. "Sorry Maki-san," Kaori said. "Maybe I should have gotten up at three in the morning." The line crept along at a snail's pace, and it was two hours before we even got to the gate, where we received the numbers 464 and 465. I only took a number because I wanted to do the same thing as the other patients. I didn't really have any illnesses, so I had to think about what I would ask Dr. Fritz to work on.

Anticipating the many hours we would have to wait made me very impatient. Even during my daily routine of twenty minutes of meditation, I sometimes get so impatient that I check my watch to see if the time is up. I decided it would be good discipline for me to be patient as we waited in line.

Nonetheless, the six hours until Rubens showed up were very long and boring for me. I wished that I had brought some book to read or even a portable chess game, but looking around the large hall, I saw hardly anyone reading, and, of course, no one was playing games. Waiting was spiritual and emotional preparation for meeting with Dr. Fritz.

Around two in the afternoon, Rubens and his wife finally arrived, and Rubens channeled Dr. Fritz as usual. The day before, at Cesarina's mansion, Rubens' wife told David that Rubens had been sick in bed all day, but today he looked well rested and completely recovered. He was very alive and enthusiastic.

He began by working on the patients in the operating room. The first was Marcelo's mother, who had had brain surgery the previous Monday when the Discovery Channel was filming the clinic. Marcelo, her physician son, was with her. I thanked Marcelo again for letting us visit their home last week, and then we watched Dr. Fritz treat his mother again. He looked closely at the new CAT scan and X-rays of her brain, holding them up to the fluorescent lights on the ceiling. As Marcelo had feared, the cancer cells had spread, so Dr. Fritz told them she would need another operation the following week.

I wanted to talk with Marcelo about the details of his mother's condition, but Dr. Fritz had already moved on to the next bed, in which a cute baby lay. Because this operation looked very unusual and interesting, I chose to stay and watch rather than interview Marcelo further.

Dr. Fritz is very fond of babies and children. He always makes them his first priority. Even if a child has the number 700, he treats him or her first. The mother lay down on the bed next to her baby. She had a worried look on her face. I was glad that Alice, the part-time English teacher and volunteer nurse, was working today. She whispered to me, "This baby boy is blind. First one eye lost the cornea, and now the other has tissue blockage." I wondered how Dr. Fritz would operate on this tiny baby's eye.

To my surprise, he asked the mother to hold her baby's hand, and began operating on the healthy eyes of the mother! The baby didn't receive any treatment. Perhaps Dr. Fritz noted my surprise, because the hand that held the scalpel stopped and he looked up at me and began to explain in English. "This is one of the most difficult operations to perform. This is how to treat the mother for her child. I cut here, freeing the tissue in the mother. In two or three days, there will be no more tissue in his eye. Then this baby boy can see. This kind of operation hasn't been performed before. The mother and her baby have a very similar DNA structure, so through the hand-holding, the change in the DNA can be transferred to the baby at the speed of light."

Then he turned back and continued moving the scalpel on the surface of the mother's eye. The operation was successfully completed, and the nurse placed some cotton gauze over the mother's eye. Dr. Fritz seemed to be in a great mood.

Before he went on to the next operation, he said in English, "Let me explain to you a little more about the treatment of mothers and babies." I got my cassette recorder out in a hurry and turned it on. "Some children I operate on, others no, because they are too small. Not because of the size of the operation, but because I feel sorry for the baby. So I do it on the mother. Generally there is a blood tie. Mother's green eye, father's curly hair, everything genetic. Later you will learn that these chromosomal genetic associations can transport energy. There is a chain that is electronically interlinked. You have to alter a piece. Not the whole thing, just a piece. Remember the formula: adenine, guanine. One triggers the next. Change one and that's it."

"But if someone has a genetic disease, their genetic code is in all their cells. Then what?" I asked.

"You have to study a little bit more," he said. "One DNA talks to another DNA. A Chinese-American researcher discovered this in 1933. He was ridiculed at the time. He discovered that DNA molecules communicate with each other, saying 'Oh, you change,' and then the next one changes, too. Then the next and the next. Now you are also discovering this."

"I heard Dr. Fritz can do bone regeneration, or reconstruction, of molecules," I said.

"I have reconstructed the internal ear, the external ear, the cranium bones. I can reconstruct anything, except nerve cells.

"Except nerve cells?" I asked.

"Yes. What I'm doing here is not exactly a miracle. There is a system determining what can happen. When I can, I fix it. When I can't, I'm not going to lie to you. If I say, I will fix it and it doesn't get better, it doesn't help. I only fix it if it can get better. The disease I can't cure is the disease since birth, that which is congenital. And also the physical body that has fibrosis I can't cure, because the astral body does not have enough water for me to do anything. And some genetic diseases I can't cure, and definitely, I can do nothing for nerve cell lesions. The nerve cells that you think are so marvelous really aren't. There are things that I can't treat. I can reduce the pain. That's the most I can do."

"Thank you very much for your very interesting explanation," I said. "I don't want to steal any more of your precious time." When we arrived before eight in the morning, I was number 465. Now there were more than 800 patients waiting for Dr. Fritz in the large hall. He had only treated two people so far, and I didn't want to delay him.

He went on to the next patient, a heavy, middle-aged man. Dr. Fritz made an incision in the man's shoulder and inserted a clamp. Then he put a scalpel deep into the man's fat layers and moved it incredibly quickly. As I watched, astonished, he removed a chunk of flesh about one inch in diameter, perhaps a tumor, from the man's shoulder, and handed it to the nurse. She put the chunk into a small bottle of alcohol and gave it to the patient. Five minutes later, the patient left the operating room with his souvenir in hand, thanking everyone enthusiastically over and over.

How do doctors and specialists view this kind of rough operation? In the video, psychiatrist Eleanor Luzes says: "I have ten years' experience researching parapsychology. I'm trained as a psychiatrist and psychoanalyst, and also did years of surgical practice during my post-graduate medical studies. During the two or three months that I have been in contact with Dr. Fritz, I have observed that his surgical procedures are absolutely absurd. For example, I saw him perform one surgery where he inserted a needle through the occipital foramen of a woman in an extremely violent manner. The way he moved the needle in that place would have damaged various structures and that person should certainly have died, because this area controls breathing. Or at the very least she would have been totally incapacitated, not able to get up or walk. But this didn't happen. I saw other surgical procedures, like for arthritis in the knee. The way in which he used the instruments made absolutely no sense at all—stretching, pulling, twisting. In no way would these be normal procedures to solve anything. Another thing that got my attention is that after any of these neurosurgeries, it should be impossible for the patient to be instantaneously lucid, able to talk, to walk, to get up immediately after the end of the surgery."

Dr. Arnold Mindel, the founder of process-oriented psychology and the author of *Dream Body Work,* explains it this way: "Well, I can see it in the change in people. Ahead of time, they have this big consternation on their face. They are upset. They are in pain. Afterwards you see the lines on their faces disappear and they start sparkling. They feel better. There is hope. What I saw was the spirit of Dr. Fritz working through the healer to change the dream body. The dream body is the experience we have of dreams, which appear to pattern our body experiences. For example, if you have a tumor, you may experience that tumor as a fist or knot, something very tight. You may be dreaming about a fight. The dream body is the idea that behind the fist or tumor is a conflict or power inside yourself. The spirit of Dr. Fritz goes in and changes those patterns around, as people can also do by themselves, but they usually don't believe enough in themselves."

Dr. Fritz finished all the operations and was moving to the main clinic room when he noticed me again and said, "The operation itself is rather easy for me. The most difficult thing is opening up the heart of the people. I am not curing this or that mechanical malfunction of the physical body."

An hour later, I got thirsty, so I went out the gate and bought some mango juice from a street vendor. Then Kaori walked up to me with a very serious expression on her face. She had gone to the clinic room to observe further treatments. "Maki-san," she said, "a terrible thing is happening!"

"What's up Kaori-san? You look very serious. Did the teacher scold you?"

"Yes! That's exactly right! About two hundred patients waiting in the clinic room were talking and making noise, even after Dr. Fritz began the injections."

"Ah-ha. So he got angry, huh?"

"Yes, he was furious! It scared me. I had to escape and find you so I could talk to you about it."

"That's interesting," I said. "Let's go and see what's happening."

When we got back inside, we saw that Dr. Fritz's face looked quite different. His half-opened eyes were sharper, his low husky voice was louder, and he was still yelling at the patients in the room. He was far from the image of an angel, saint, or holy man. Most of the patients stood looking at the floor, looking sorry for having been noisy. Of course, Dr. Fritz was scolding them in Portuguese, so I couldn't understand what he said, but I assumed it was something like, "Did you folks come here just to talk and make noise? God gave you a disease so you could have a chance to learn and grow through your pain!"

It reminded me of similar scenes in the video. In one, an old blind man tried to cut in front of others. Dr. Fritz was enraged. "People who wish to get in first, get out of here! I'm not kidding! The ones who can't see push to get up front." To the old man, he said: "You're acting like children, pushing to get in front of each other, just wanting to be cured. This is stupidity!" The old man said, "I am blind. I live far away. It took two days to get here." Dr. Fritz said, "You are blind?" The old man said, "Yes. I can't see a thing." Then Dr. Fritz said, "Listen, I'm going to tell you something." The old man interrupted again, "I came here to be cured." Dr. Fritz said, "You came here to be cured? Wait a minute. Come here."

Then Dr. Fritz brought a small child over to where the old man stood and said to him, "Put your hand here. What is this?"

"A child," the old man replied.

"You know what's in his ear? A tumor. How old is he?" he

asked the boy's mother. "Three years old," she answered. "How old are you?" he asked the blind man.

He said, "I am sixty-five."

"He is three and you have already lived sixty-five years, so you have to wait and ask God for him to be cured. You shouldn't be looking for your cure. You should be looking for others to be cured."

The old man said, "I want everyone here to be cured."

Dr. Fritz became really angry and explained to the camera, "Compassion for others. Faith. This is what they don't know. Cutting in line to get in front. Why? Talking all the time instead of praying." He turned to the patients. "You are crazy coming here just to talk. Why don't you shut your mouth and think about God? Some days something impressive happens. Everyone is united, really like brothers. 'How are you doing? Any better? Look what I brought you. Let me drive you home.' We are making brotherhood, joining people who love each other. This is what I want you to share, how you should treat each other. 'Oh doctor, can you cure me?' It's not like that. You have to say 'Doctor, look at him because he's not feeling well. Doctor, look at this girl who needs treatment.'

"Remember yourself as the last one, not the first. Then I cure more quickly. Like this one, who waited three months until one day I said to him, 'Now I will cure you.' Because he had faith and let others go in front of him. He wasn't thinking of himself anymore, only of God. Then it was easy to cure. My hand is nothing. God's hand is more important. Did you see the woman with brain surgery? Did you feel sorry for her? No. Did you feel happy that she was cured? That's it. That's the social relationship. It's all one thing, one head, one body, one way to live."

Back in the clinic room, after half an hour of scolding and preaching, Dr. Fritz gave one piece of cotton gauze to each person. Alice, the volunteer nurse, told me that tonight, before these patients went to sleep, they were to put the gauze on the diseased part of their body for about thirty minutes and pray for a cure.

Then about ten of the nurses and workers got together in the clinic room and formed two lines facing each other. Lifting their arms, they created an archway of energy beneath their healing hands. The patients who had received cotton gauze from Dr. Fritz walked beneath the arches and went back home. They had lower numbers than us, so they must have waited in line since at least seven in the morning. I was pretty sure that not all of them had been noisy, that a lot of them had been quiet all the time. But because of joint responsibility, after waiting eleven hours for their turn, they had to be sent home with just a single piece of gauze. I felt deeply sorry for them. I couldn't look directly into their faces, but I know how disappointed they must have felt.

Ironically, because these two hundred patients were sent home early, our turn came sooner than we expected. When it did, Kaori told Dr. Fritz, "Those annoying noises in my ear haven't gone away."

"I will try my best," he said, "But if this has more of a karmic cause, maybe you would do better to live with it and learn something from it." Again, he injected her very quickly behind her ear.

Then it was my turn. Since nothing was wrong with my body, I told him half-jokingly, "I sleep too much every day." He laughed and injected me lightly behind the neck. It was obviously an astral body injection, because I felt no pain or pinch at all on my skin. He said, "Now six hours sleep a day is enough for you." He laughed and we shook hands. Then we said good-bye and left through the gate.

It was my last opportunity to see the clinic. When I looked back at the broken windows and peeling paint on the walls, all sorts of memories came flooding up and I became very emotional, as though some unknown energy had touched me deep inside.

Thanks to Dr. Fritz's anger at the two hundred patients who were kicked out, we were able to arrive at the planetarium just in time for the book signing. In the lobby, Dr. Moura, wearing a fancy black evening dress, was almost finished signing books before going to the stage to deliver her special lecture in Portuguese. Everyone in front of us held a copy of her newly published book, *Transformation of Consciousness*. I thought it would be good manners to buy her book, even though it was in Portuguese and I couldn't read it, so I quickly bought a copy. It had a beautifully illustrated cover.

When our turn came, I told her: "I was in your workshop at the ITA conference in Manaus. It was a great presentation."

"Thank you very much," she said. "How did you know about the book signing here?"

"David Sonnenschein, the movie director, told us about it yesterday. Would you please autograph my book?"

"Of course, but what are you going to do with a book written in Portuguese?"

"When I go back to Colorado, I'll find someone to translate it. But if possible, I would really like to interview you about the Dr. Fritz phenomenon."

"Is that right? That's why you are here, isn't it? But I'm about to start my lecture in the planetarium, so I can't do it right now."

"We're leaving for the United States the day after tomorrow in the evening. Would you have a little time before that?"

"I have about one hour I can spend with you tomorrow evening. Can you come to my house at Ipanema Beach?"

We were so happy to hear this that Kaori and I did a high-five in front of her table to express our joy. Then I read the autograph she put in the book: "My dear Maki-san, I hope you can find every answer to your questions on this trip. Love and Peace, Gilda Moura."

To celebrate our unexpected success in getting an interview with Dr. Moura, we decided to have dinner at a nearby sushi bar. It was quite tiny, with space for only five people. As we sat eating our sushi and drinking a local brand of beer, I thought how this trip had gone far better than I could have imagined. Suddenly Kaori began laughing. "Maki-san. Don't you think we are kind of funny?"

"What's funny about us?" I asked.

"We've been in Copacabana Beach for ten days now. This is a world-famous beach resort, and we haven't gone swimming even once."

"That's right," I said. "We haven't even touched the sand on the beach, even though we've been staying at a beachfront hotel with an ocean view."

"Maybe we should call ourselves Fritz nuts!" Kaori said.

UFOs, Dr. Fritz, and ETs

December 3

Today we were to meet a woman named Baixinha. I had heard about her a few days before leaving Colorado. In Boulder, there are so many healers that people say if you throw a stone at the downtown mall, it most likely will hit one. But among Boulder healers, there is an extraordinary woman named Mimi, who has been dubbed a healer of healers. She is a twenty-year veteran of the field, and visits Brazil nearly every year to teach Rolfing and other healing techniques.

When I was introduced to Mimi at my restaurant, Sushi Zanmai, I told her about meeting Dr. Fritz. "Dr. Fritz is more than amazing," she said, "But if you are going to Rio de Janeiro again, I strongly recommend you meet Baixinha. I've gone to Brazil six times to teach, but my real purpose was to meet Baixinha and learn from her. The last time I was there, a young black woman was brought to her. The woman was crying and thrashing around violently on the floor. Baixinha simply put her hand on the woman's forehead, and all of a sudden the patient became quiet."

I have heard that Baixinha usually lives deep in the jungle in the mountains, and is the priestess of a ceremonial cult called Umbanda. Every once in a while, though, she visits Rio and has healing sessions with clients there.

Luckily, our hectic schedule and Baixinha's visit to Rio overlapped. In the morning, Kaori and I took a taxi to the hillside house where Baixinha was staying. The woman who greeted us at the door was very tiny and had long graceful hair down to her hips. She spoke no English but, using gestures and reading each others' vibrations, we communicated nearly perfectly. Through her front window, we could see the gigantic white statue of Jesus Christ on Corcovado.

When we met, she was carrying a book called *Hands of Light* by the American healer Barbara Brennan, who used to be a NASA scientist. Baixinha opened the book and pointed to a color illustration of the human auric field. She seemed to be trying to say she could see these fields. Then she stepped back a few paces and closed her eyes halfway, as if she were asleep, and looked my body over. With a smile, she stuck her thumb in the air and said, "*Muito bom*," which means "very good" in Portuguese. Then she turned to Kaori and repeated the same thing, but afterwards touched Kaori's lower abdomen and said something more. She seemed to be saying that this area was not functioning well. Kaori was surprised, and said, "How did she see this? My family has a history of colon disease. At birth my colon was very weak. Just this morning, I started to feel something was wrong in my lower abdomen. I'm really impressed." Once again, I was convinced that there are things that normal people can't see, but that people like Dr. Fritz or Baixinha can.

Then Baixinha led me to a nearby room. Here, the tables and shelves were filled with dozens of symbols, sacred stones, statues, and two simple massage tables. She asked me to lie down on the massage table and close my eyes. As she began her healing work, she sang in a high-pitched, bird-like voice, making sounds like "eeya karimpe ne nakabo kuro krina misa nira." Later, I was told this was a sacred song used to communicate with Caboclo, a nature spirit of the Amazonian Indians and the primary spirit in the Umbanda religion, of which Baixinha was a leader.

In his book *Religion in Latin America*, Dr. Tomio Fujita, a professor at Rikkyo University in Tokyo, writes: "Umbanda is a religion that came from the lost continent of Lemuria. The survivors of Lemuria escaped to India and founded Hinduism. There are several legends that say this ancient religion still remains in

Africa, as well. The word *umbanda* comes from the Sanskrit word *aum-banda*. *Aum* means metaphysical sacredness, and banda means continuous movement."

At the end of our healing session, Baixinha communicated by gestures that she saw lots of nature spirits dancing joyfully around me. She began singing again, "La la la la," and with her hands in the air, danced like a fairy.

After Kaori's session, she said, "Wow, it works so well. My lower abdomen feels noticeably better." Whether a witch doctor, shaman, or magician, Baixinha gave me the impression that she could be an authentic example of any of these.

After finishing our sessions, Baixinha showed us some photographs of Umbanda ceremonies conducted deep in the mountainous jungle where she lives. Some of the photographs showed men and women dressed in pure white, praying and dancing ecstatically. In one picture, people participated in a cleansing ritual underneath a waterfall. Among them I recognized one man with a long white beard as the priest of Santo Daime Church, Alex Polari, who conducted the ceremony in Manaus at the ITA conference. Then I realized that these unusual religions were somehow connected.

In the late afternoon, we went to see Dr. Gilda Moura, who lives in a luxurious condominium on exclusive Ipanema Beach. Her penthouse suite has an outside verandah and a deck with a big hot tub. The living room is filled with beautiful and artistic furniture from all over the world. Kaori noticed a table in the middle of the living room and said, "I just saw that exact same table in Cairo, Egypt."

While we sat sipping delicious Brazilian coffee brought by Dr. Moura's maid, she came in and greeted us, wearing casual clothes. "Thank you for granting us an interview on such short notice," I said. As I prepared the tape recorder, she informed me, "I only have an hour and a half until the next appointment, so we need to talk efficiently."

While her face gave the impression of a highly intellectual person, I could also feel her warmth and big heart. She seemed to be a wonderful scholar; her voice was clear and persuasive and full of confidence. I am not the ablest interviewer, and sometimes ask irrelevant questions, but she always answered me very sincerely and comprehensively. This is the text of the interview:

"What is your main profession?"

"I am a clinical psychologist, and a founder of the Altered State of Consciousness Research Center."

"Why did you begin researching the Dr. Fritz phenomenon?"

"That's a long story. While I was working as a psychologist, I became interested in paranormal phenomena, because in this field everything is stronger, more complex. So if you are searching for something unusual, you can measure it more easily. That's what interested me."

"At the ITA conference in Manaus, you and Dr. Norman Don gave a joint presentation of your study, including Dr. Fritz's brain waves. How did you obtain those?"

"I always felt some kind of light on the face of those people when they went into trance states, as if they were in a hyper-aroused trance. I began to think that I would like to measure it to see if it was just my impression, or if there was really something going on in the brain. One day there was a Transpersonal Conference in Rio and Dr. Don was giving a talk and a slide show about his lab and describing the kind of research he was doing there. He is co-director of a brain function laboratory at the University of Illinois at Chicago. After the conference, I said to him that if he had the kind of cutting-edge technology that could measure brain waves, then I had the people—the psychic surgeons and all sorts of other people who exhibit paranormal phenomenon. That's how we began our joint research."

"And how long have you been doing this kind of research?"

"It took about five years of traveling around Brazil. We went to Bahia, Recife, Mato Grosso, and others. We took videos and blood samples of the healers and patients. Then we measured the brain waves of the healers."

"When did you meet Dr. Fritz?"

"At first, we took videos of Edson Queiroz, the last famous Dr. Fritz, who died five years ago. He was performing surgeries on the stage of a theater. For me, it was amazing because I felt similar sensations as I did from those who had experienced some UFO phenomenon. That was the first time I met Edson Queiroz. The second time, I went to see him in Recife and took all our video equipment. Something began happening. There were physicians and patients all around, and he began calling to me and showing me what he was doing. This was the first time the entity, the personality of Dr. Fritz, talked directly to me."

"Who was the second medium you researched who channeled Dr. Fritz?"

"A medium named Mauricio who lives in the state of Mato Grosso do Sul. He was not as known as Edson or Rubens, but he also channeled Dr. Fritz. About 500 patients came to see him at his clinic every day."

"Was there any common ground or similarity between Mauricio and Edson Queiroz?"

"Oh yes. When Mauricio was with Dr. Fritz, I had doubts about him because, being a scientist, I had to ask myself, Is he really channeling a 'spirit'? He was a totally different personality and person. He didn't recognize me or anyone else [who had met Dr. Fritz before]. After an hour, though, he went deeper into his trance and began speaking more German than before and talking with the wife of the anthropologist who had researched Edson Queiroz for many years. So she knew Dr. Fritz for many years through her husband. Then Mauricio looked at her and said, "How long it's been since I've seen you!" He recognized her. Then he began talking with me the same way Edson had done, explaining in the same words. Then, through Mauricio, he told me how to continue my research on him."

"So what do you think about Rubens?"

"Rubens is very different from the historical mediums of the German doctor's 'spirit.' Before Rubens, most of the mediums were physically more heavy. Rubens has a lighter physical constitution. He is also an engineer, which helps with the research. One day when I was doing research on Rubens, I brought a physician friend with me. After Rubens treated him, I was taking a photograph of them together when Dr. Fritz told me, 'Please focus on my hand. You will get pictures of light coming in.' I tried to take a few pictures that would show his hand clearly. Here is one of them." She showed us a picture of Dr. Fritz putting his right hand over the physicians left shoulder and smiling. Diagonally, from above his hand, I could see that light was coming in.

"The figure of Dr. Fritz in Kardecism is considered a manifestation of a spirit during the First World War, but if you observe a little more closely, from another point of view—for example, as a frequency—the mediums I have researched—Rubens and others— give the sensation not of seeing a 'spirit' but of seeing a very strong light, usually in yellow tones. Therefore Fritz could be considered not only as a 'spirit' but also a code, an opening to a frequency. Dr. Eleanor Luzes said, 'In reality, Fritz functions as a giant particle accelerator. To understand what he does, one needs to know quantum physics.'"

I was amazed at the photos of light coming through Rubens, so I asked, "Do you have photos of other channelers?"

"Yes. I took some when I researched Antônio, the medium of Dr. Ricardo. Dr. Ricardo used an electric disk saw to chop up patients' backs. You can see the blood is spread out all over. It was so intense. I have a video of the operation. We showed it at several conferences, to get more feedback about the phenomenon."

"Just a moment," I said. "Dr. Ricardo is the same 'spirit' who sometimes appears during Rubens' treatments. Is this the same Dr. Ricardo who likes to cut and open up the body?"

"Yes, we are probably talking about the same 'spirit.' But when Antônio channeled Dr. Ricardo, he told me that I could take photos. There is a belief in the town that the energy comes from a space laboratory through a tube of light. So I took a few photos, one right after the operation where he used the electric disk saw, and a tube of light came out in the pictures, in a spiral shape."

She showed me the photo of a half-naked man lying face down on a bed. His back was deeply cut and the wall was covered with blood. It looked liked something from a Hollywood horror movie. But near the patient's leg a bundle of light came down from above in a spiral shape. Dr. Moura pointed to it and said, "Look at this. There a light was coming in from somewhere in the universe. At first I thought this was from the negative becoming over-exposed, so I took it to a lab to check. They proved that this was a real image on the film, not a malfunction of the camera or any-thing like that."

"Are there many more channelers like this in Brazil?"

"Yes. I have come across many interesting trance surgeons and healers in my research. One is Dr. João de Abadiani. He is a real doctor, but he does surgery when he channels the 'spirit' of Santo Inácio. In his case, he sometimes has the patients, five of them, stand together in a row. Then he operates on the first patient while they are all standing. Then, all of a sudden, the scar from the surgery can appear on all of them. I was there with a research team. They all took photos of it." She showed me the photos.

"This is beyond me," I said. "It's unbelievable."

"I am a psychologist. I am a scientific researcher, not a cheap writer in the tabloids. I'm just telling you the exact experience I had on this research trip. Now I'd like to introduce you to one more trance surgeon. His name is Venâncio, and he also lives in Bahia. He uses a pen in his operations."

"You mean like this writing pen?"

"Yes. He draws a line on the skin with the pen wherever he operates. Then, he puts a bandage over it, no incision. Venâncio did an operation on my belly using his pen. He put a long bandage on my belly and asked me not to remove it for one week. But three days later, my belly was getting a lot better and I wanted to swim, so I ignored his warning and took the bandage off. Then to my surprise, where he drew the line with his pen, there was a scarring as if I had had stitches."

As she said this, she showed me another picture of her in a bikini. I could see the scar of the vertical incision on her belly, about seven inches long. It looked like a welt. It was undoubtedly real.

Kaori and I were having trouble digesting all these new pieces of information, coming so fast one after another. We were stunned and a little lost. But Dr. Moura continued without a pause: "The strange thing is, one week later, these scars disappeared totally. Nothing remains."

"Dr. Moura, you and Dr. Norman Don measured the brain waves of those people, right?"

"Yes. Amazingly, we found that the mediums of German doctors all had a similar frequency when they went into trance. About Rubens, he has a wonderful alpha wave when he is just relaxed. Alpha is the wave your brain emits when you are in a peaceful state, relaxed. But there is a special brain wave frequency that the so-called German 'spirit' doctors exhibit, including Rubens. When he channels Dr. Fritz, the brain wave goes up to more than forty hertz. Normal human beings can go up to thirty hertz. At all nineteen points we tested, we found a fast, low-amplitude frequency that reaches forty hertz. That is a state in which you are more alert, concentrated, and objective, more able to make decisions and solve problems. Our brain, normally, only goes up to thirty hertz.

"How can this research help us? I think that as soon we understand our minds in these states of control and access other levels that we don't normally use—levels that can cure, that can anesthetize, that can prevent proliferation of bacteria—it will be very important for our medical practitioners and for individuals to learn. When people learn how to reach the forty-hertz brain wave, that will be so important for our growth. This will help us learn to make a better world."

"So it's the forty hertz brain wave that gives Dr. Fritz the ability to give 'superhuman' treatments. Is that right?"

"No, it appears to be one condition, but we are just starting. According to others' published studies, the only people who could go over forty hertz were Indian yoga practitioners in *samadhi* state. According to our research, the brain waves of UFO experiencers can also go above forty hertz. But you have to see the picture of the brain mapping of the nineteen points we measured on the brain of these trance surgeons."

"So who do you think Dr. Fritz really is?"

"I said in a presentation at a UFO conference at the Massachusetts Institute of Technology in Boston that the German doctors operated similarly to the aliens in abductees' episodes. When I say an alien or being, I'm not saying someone who comes from another planet. I'm talking about a kind of manifestation, a kind of frequency. And when Arigó started to channel the 'spirit' of Dr. Fritz, it was the same year as the modern era of UFO sightings started."

"When is the UFO's modern Era?" I asked.

"It started in 1947. So it is the same period that UFOs began to appear on our planet frequently. At the same time, the 'spirit' of Dr. Fritz began appearing in Brazil. Isn't that something to think about?"

"Maybe they started to expose themselves more directly to the human consciousness."

"I think that the aliens are probably using the structure and paradigm of Dr. Fritz, who is a German historical figure, so people can easily understand and relate to it and accept it. But one of the big differences between Rubens and the other mediums of German doctors is that besides being a medium, Rubens is also a channeler. So he is being used to convey messages about big changes in the future and stuff, as are the other channelers around the world."

"What is the main purpose of this ET group coming back to Earth?" I asked.

"Because prior to the change of the millennium, they needed to encourage and promote the evolution of human consciousness. I wrote about this in the book you bought yesterday. I describe it as a mass initiation, because that's how I saw it at the time. But now, I see things differently. It is not only a mass initiation of human consciousness, it is much broader than that. It is going to effect the physical level too."

"You mean a change in the DNA code or something like that?"

"Yes, but I really do not know how this is going to happen. We need further research."

"If there is going to be such a big change in human history, what kind of preparations do we need to make?"

"I think first of all, do what many people are already doing, give love. You have to think, talk, and express yourself in a loving way. So don't hide the feeling in your heart, be transparent."

"That sounds easy, but it might be hard to do."

"Yes. Human beings have conditioning and a big ego. Most people think and say one thing and do another. Besides, we have fear. Fear is the worst thing. Inside we have so many bad memories: memories of war, killing each other, black magic, hatred, and so on."

While she answered this last question, the doorbell rang. To our regret, her next guest had arrived. The hour and a half had passed so quickly. We were there to talk about Dr. Fritz, but the conversation had gone so far beyond that. As we said good-bye, she gave us a few copies of her precious photos, which really thrilled me. But I discovered that the photos of brain waves were not among them. Although I thought it was impudent to ask, I did. "Is it possible for you to give us copies of the photos of Dr. Fritz's brain waves?"

"This is not my personal commodity," she said. "They are from the joint research conducted by me and Dr. Don. But if you'll wait a minute, I'll call him in Chicago and ask him what he thinks about it."

As the new guest waited in the living room, she called Dr. Don. He told her he had one condition: if we were not using it for scientific presentations to academics, then we could use the photos. I was as happy as a kid who had just gotten a ton of candy. We thanked her and left the house.

After returning to the hotel, Kaori went to bed early. This was our last evening in Brazil, and I was left alone. I walked across the road to the beach by myself. The tourists had gone, so hardly anyone was there. I walked down the beach and, for the first time since coming to Rio de Janeiro, I touched the ocean. The waves and whitecaps shone white, reflecting the line of hotel lights. It was beautiful, and I sat down on the damp sand and watched the waves come and go for a long, long time.

I thought about human beings and other living creatures repeating the cycles of death and birth uncountable times, like those waves endlessly coming and going. And within the span of eternity, millions of stars and planets were also being born and dying millions of times.

In the southern hemisphere, the water in the toilet drains in a spiral in a direction opposite to the way it drains in the southern hemisphere. The extraordinary energy of the southern hemisphere surrounded me, and I began to feel very sentimental and emotional.

In the beginning, I had gone to the ITA conference simply out of curiosity. But it had led me to so much over such a long period of time that it was as though the conference had been going on continuously for months. Tomorrow, it would truly end. I thought about the conference's name—transpersonal psychology—and realized that the changes I had gone through since I first decided to attend were truly transformational. This hadn't just been an academic experience for me, but a life-changing one. Without too much effort, my soul had a chance to grow a little.

Suddenly, I was struck with a deep desire to see Dr. Fritz again. I realized I had not really had a chance to thank him from my heart. Yes, tomorrow, just once more before leaving Brazil, I would go see him again.

As that thought passed through my mind, I heard the soothing sound of the hummingbird in my ears.

Your Face is the Face of God

December 4

In the morning, we hiked to the top of the hill in Corcovado, one of the biggest tourist attractions in the city. I say "hiked," but most of the way we rode on a Swiss-made cable car, so it was more like sightseeing.

The car was full of tourists snapping pictures. We had been here for two weeks, but on the last day before returning to the United States, we were finally acting like tourists. In a way, I felt sort of righteous for having spent all our time doing research, but now I was content to be doing something "normal."

At the summit is a gigantic statue of Jesus Christ that overlooks all of Rio de Janeiro, as though blessing the city. The statue seems several times larger than it appears on postcards. Usually, popular tourist attractions look very cheap and artificial when you see them for yourself, but this statue of Jesus was exceptional. It made my heart feel like it was vibrating. The entire hill, shaped like a spindle, seemed like an antenna designed to receive sacred vibrations from the universe.

Kaori and I spontaneously began silently praying in the way we had ever since our Peru trip the year before. In our minds, we repeated the words, "May peace prevail on the earth." Praying like this, I felt I was connecting to the big heart engraved on the breast of the statue of Christ, and I felt a pleasurable sensation throughout my body. I thought to myself that Jesus Christ must have been a great spiritual person. Nowadays, there is a lot of doomsday talk about the years 1999 and 2000, but actually, we are simply counting the years since Jesus's birth. If he were born ten years later, or not at all, the Western calendar would be quite different. Thinking about this, I felt kind of silly. As a Japanese whose family has been committed to Buddhism for four hundred years, why should I be concerned with the number of a year based on Jesus's birth? I began to feel like I was just playing with numbers. Why should the year 2000 matter at all?

After lunch, Kaori went shopping for souvenirs and I took a taxi to the Penha District, at the intersection of Rua Quito and Rua Couto, to see Dr. Fritz. I had grown accustomed to the scenes outside the taxi window, and seeing them once again made me feel a little nostalgic. At the moment I arrived, Rubens and his wife, Rita, drove into the parking lot. I was glad to see them come in a simple midsized American car instead of a Rolls Royce or Mercedes Benz. I ran to the parking lot to meet them and told them, "This is my last time here. Tonight I'm returning to the States."

Maybe it was because we were alone in the huge parking lot, apart from the pressures of his work and the endless lines of patients, that Rubens seemed so at ease and spoke so frankly with me then. He told me how much he had adored Japan since childhood. My curiosity, which I had been doing a good job of suppressing until then, got the better of me, and knowing I wouldn't get another chance, I asked him the question that had been on my mind all that time.

"Rubens, last time I was here, I heard the story about Christopher Reeve, who played Superman in the movies. Did Dr. Fritz actually do something for him?"

"I have been asked that by many people," he said. "Actually, I went to New York in June, because I was invited. I did a treatment at Mr. Reeve's house, but we had a problem. He didn't trust Dr. Fritz a hundred percent. For him, I think, Dr. Fritz is just one of many who are trying to cure him."

"So did you do an operation?"

"Yes. Dr. Fritz did one simple operation, but during the operation even my wife, who I brought along as a helper, wasn't allowed to come inside the operating room. She had to wait in the car. I thought, 'For this kind of treatment, you need total faith in the spirit.'"

"A few weeks ago, I saw Christopher Reeve on television, and he looked pretty healthy, like he was getting better, and I heard that he was going to be directing a television drama. Do you think there has been any positive effect from Dr. Fritz's treatment?"

"Yes, certainly there has. In fact, I have been invited to New York next year to do a more radical operation."

"Are you going to go?"

"I don't know. I haven't decided yet. In order to regenerate his spinal cord, it's going to take at least two weeks. Besides, damaged nerve cells are kind of difficult, even for Dr. Fritz. When I think about the thousands of patients who are relying on Dr. Fritz every day at this clinic, then sometimes I feel it is better to treat the thousands of patients here than to cure one superstar."

"I intend to write a book about my experiences with the Dr. Fritz phenomenon. If this happens, do you have any message for the Japanese people?"

"I am pretty sure that you can convey the message of Dr. Fritz in a good way. My personal desire is to inspire the Japanese to begin full-scale research on me and the Dr. Fritz phenomenon. If they do, they will discover a lot of fruitful medical technology."

"If that happens, would you visit Japan?"

"Of course. I would be glad to. I have been studying science for many years as an engineer. I think it is a total waste if no one comes to do research and discover something. This thing about 'No, this doesn't exist' is absurd. Imagine if I went to my engineering class and said, 'Look, you are not going to study electromagnetic waves, because you can't see electromagnetic waves. And if you can't see them then they don't exist.' It's absurd! It's very verifiable, so you have to do research to verify it."

"Yes, I think so too. I feel a little sorry that I'm not a scientist. If I were, maybe I could write a more persuasive book."

"No, no, no. Please write freely in your own way. But Dr. Fritz told me I am the last one on this planet who is going to work as Dr. Fritz. And I'm only going to be here for four more years. So during that time, I really hope that this technology of the spirit can be of use to human beings."

153

"I'd like to ask Dr. Fritz something directly, also."

"Oh yes, I don't see any problem with that. As long as it's okay with you to ask your questions while he's treating patients."

Then Rubens' wife, Rita, came to fetch him. Rubens said, "I'm sorry. Everyone is waiting for me so I need to go. Good luck on your book."

"I'd really like to thank you for everything," I told him.

Today, again, there were nearly a thousand patients gathered to see Dr. Fritz. Luckily, quite a few of them could speak simple English. Perhaps some of them had heard from the nurses that I was interviewing patients, because before I went looking for them, they came to me to talk about their experiences with Dr. Fritz. This was a big change from the first day I came, half a year ago. At that time, except for Rubens, no one could speak English.

I will share parts of three of these interviews here. The first was with a young man and his wife, who was in a wheelchair: "My name is Felipe and my wife is Ana Maria. I have been suffering for six years from migraine headaches that no one has been able to find a cause for. But since I started coming here for injections, most of the pain has disappeared. My wife has suffered heavily with a serious skin disease, but she is getting better also. Her dermatologist is so surprised. He can't understand how it became so much better so quickly."

The second interview was with a middle-aged man who was quite good-natured and friendly: "My name is Vidor. My daughter's name is Joana. She is eight years old. She had a brain tumor, so she was emotionally unstable and had very high blood pressure. Besides that, she suffered from an overeating syndrome. But Dr. Fritz performed brain surgery on her, and then all of her symptoms were totally cured. Her blood pressure is normal, her diet is regular, and she's emotionally stable. The other day she received an award in a composition contest in her school."

Interview number three was with an older gentleman dressed in a respectable suit: "My name is Sérgio. I'm a conductor of an orchestra in Rio. Maybe because I've been reading tiny musical notes for many years, my eyesight became so bad that I couldn't see practically anything anymore. I don't know the name of this disease in English, but I have been coming here for two months. The other day I went to the eye doctor for a checkup. Before coming here, I had only ten percent vision. Now he said it is up to fifty percent. Dr. Fritz is a truly wonderful doctor."

Of course, if people who came there for treatment didn't get positive results, they wouldn't come back for more treatment. So it is difficult to say with confidence that everyone is getting better there.

Myself, if I get appendicitis, I'll most likely get an operation at a modern hospital in the United States rather than going to Dr. Fritz. I really don't want to give the impression that Dr. Fritz is an almighty god who can cure the incurable. That would be an exaggeration and a sign of blind adulation. I don't want people who read this book to rush to Rio on a tour bus or for some rich person to offer tons of money to gain privileged access to Dr. Fritz. The Dr. Fritz phenomenon is happening in Brazil, and nowhere else. Something about that nation called forth this phenomenon, and the poor people of Brazil desperately need the healing it provides. It would be a shame if they were excluded because people from elsewhere suddenly flooded Dr. Fritz's clinic.

But there is an important reason for me to write this book, and that is to convey Dr. Fritz's message to the people of Japan and America. What is that message? I'll let the answer come straight from the mouth of Dr. Fritz. I last interviewed him while he was treating a hundred people. He never once stopped the injections, even while answering my questions into the microphone.

"Dr. Fritz, could you explain the energy you are using?"

"When I treat patients, I use the energy inside the patient. Everybody has this kind of energy in their cells. Inside the cells, the name of the organism is the mitochondrion [a micro-thread inside the cytoplasm of the cell]. I use the energy of the mitochondrion to treat my patients. The energy I use is closer to the concept of *chi* energy, as they call it in Chinese; or *prana*, as the Indian people call it; or *ki*, as the Japanese call it. But I use this energy very intensively."

"Is it possible to train ourselves to use this kind of energy? What kind of training can you recommend?"

"During Rubens' training period, I taught him many different methods and asked him to practice them. Rubens has been getting better and better at using these energies and has been teaching some of these techniques in his classes."

"Would you mind teaching me one of those methods right now?"

"All right. I will teach you a simple method to increase clairvoyance. First, you need to empty your mind, or the inside of your brain. Then imagine and visualize the astral body, which has the same shape as your physical body. Then imagine that astral body filled with golden, shining energy. Then imagine there is a thick wall on both sides of your body. Then, using the arms and hands of your astral body, try to widen it, and combine this with deep breathing. If you try this, within five minutes you will feel you are getting filled up with invisible energy."

I remembered that in the video, Rubens spoke about movement and about combining the seven chakras and seven colors and seven different musical tones. I continued my questioning.

"In your opinion, are human beings improving?"

"Yes, but very slowly, like a turtle. Human beings are using their energies in more negative ways, like anger or fighting."

"To you, what is the evolution of the human being?"

"To me, the human being— including you—is like a seed. All the people here are like seeds, and in order for seeds to grow, they need water and the light of the sun and fertile soil. My job is to water the human being. This is my water." He pointed to the hypodermic needle in his hand and smiled.

"In what direction will human beings go when we grow more?"

"Evolution starts from the soul or spirit. There is only one way to develop and change the soul—to seek greater, unconditional love. When love fills up the being, the inside of the brain becomes empty. With emptiness—which means that all thinking disappears—you find God inside yourself. So you need to search for this kind of love in your heart. The key to the evolution of human consciousness is in your pocket. You are the key. You have to remember this."

"Some people are channeling information about or predicting a big change at the turn of the century, at the millennium. What do you have to say about this?"

"The year 2000 is a very crucial, important year for humankind. It is just like a gate to the next level. This is the mystical turning point which can totally change the way of being."

"How should we prepare our minds for this? Is there anything we should do or strive for?"

"Every day has the potential for major change. You can transform yourself right now, at this moment. You have to live as if every day is the year 2000, the day of transformation. You need to go deep inside your soul. Personally, I don't like the year 2000. I prefer to be here now, right at this moment."

"Kaori has something she wanted me to ask you if I got the chance. Does Dr. Fritz remember his birthday?"

"You mean my birthday? Dr. Fritz's birthday?" He laughed. "Yes, I remember."

"You see, Kaori is an astrologer, so she's interested in your birthday."

"My birthday is 1874," he said, and laughed again.

"Do you remember the date?

"It was July 1."

"Was it in the morning or evening?"

"It was fifteen minutes after 10 in the morning."

"Where was it? In Germany?"

"Yes. I was born in Munich."

"I have one last question. Do you have any message from Dr. Fritz to our friends in Japan?"

"A message to the Japanese people? Okay, I understand." As he continued to inject his patients, he began speaking almost in verse, pausing occasionally for effect:

"Try to see beyond the river…
Try to see the far horizon…
Try to see the universe beyond the soul…
Try to see the face of God just like you look into your own face…
Please find yourself…
Please discover your soul…
Please live the world of the divine every day."

Then he said, "Finally, I have a story to tell. A man woke up one morning and looked into the mirror and there was no face in the mirror looking back at him. He said, 'Oh my god, where is my face?!' Then, from far away, God answered him: 'You've got to look inside your heart very carefully and deeply. Then you will see that my face and your face are together."

Pausing for a moment, he looked at me and said, "*Obrigado*. I will see you again sometime."

I thanked him and said, "I will try my best to deliver your message."

I went around saying good-bye to all the nurses and workers I had become acquainted with, and left through the clinic's iron gates.

THE LAST EXAM FOR HUMANKIND

December 4

David's house was farther away than I thought, but Kaori and I were so absorbed in conversation about Dr. Fritz that I barely noticed.

"By the way," I asked, "is that annoying sound in your ear gone?"

"Oh, that sound," she said. "It seems to have gotten quieter, but it's still there."

"That's all right. It's proof that Dr. Fritz can't cure every disease, right?"

"Yes, but it's okay, because now I think of the noise as a kind of barometer of my inner self. When I'm in a bad mood or negative state, the sound gets bigger. When I meditate and/or feel happy, I really don't hear it much. Besides, if this is my karma, and having an affliction like this contributes to my spiritual growth, then I can live with it. But maybe I can only say this because I'm not in any pain...."

As we spoke, the taxi brought us to a community near the ocean made up of a dozen high-rise apartments. David lived on the fifth floor of a pale blue building. The beige building next door was Rubens' home. Once again, I was glad that Rubens didn't live in a big mansion with a swimming pool, tennis court, and gatekeeper.

Half an hour ago, the dazzling afternoon sun had been uncomfortably strong, but now it was a little milder. David took us out to his deck, where we could enjoy the view of the ocean and a gentle breeze. For half an hour, we just relaxed and made small talk. But when the topic came around to the prediction that

Rubens would die four years in the future, David suddenly became quite serious. I flipped on the tape recorder and began asking him questions.

"Is Dr. Fritz helping Rubens to prepare for his death?"

"Yes. In order that Rubens won't regret his life, Dr. Fritz is training him to live fully here and now. By doing that, his soul can grow and mature until the moment of his death."

"I heard that Dr. Fritz told Rubens he was going to die violently."

"Yes. Dr. Fritz's mediums are not allowed to die slowly in bed. Usually, if someone dies instantly or violently, their soul can be stuck somewhere in between, or, some say, these souls become poltergeists. But Dr. Fritz said that his spirit group is coming to retrieve Rubens' spirit at the moment of his death, so we don't have to worry about that at all. The spirit group of Dr. Fritz and Rubens are all leaving this planet in the year 2000."

"Coincidentally, more than a few New Age channelers worldwide are predicting big changes in the year 2000. Do you think there is any connection between Rubens' death and this transformation?"

"Yes. Actually, what you say is right. Once Dr. Fritz told me during an interview that Rubens' death is not a matter of personal accident. It is a big catastrophe that can affect all human beings. Humankind is facing circumstances that we have never experienced in history. But we have a very short time left to prepare for that. That's what Dr. Fritz said to me."

"What? Dr. Fritz said that? But, David, you didn't say a word about this the last time I interviewed you, at Cesarina's mansion!"

"Yes," he said. "To tell you the truth, I have hesitated to tell you this. Dr. Fritz didn't ask me not to tell anyone. It was my personal decision not to put any of this information in my video, because I didn't want to scare any viewers."

I was more than a little shocked. I recalled the words of Kinko Sensei in São Paulo when she spoke with the voice of a Japanese god: "If they say when and where this big catastrophe is going to happen, then it will be like people are living in hell." At the time, I just listened and laughed, and half thought it was a joke. But a message about the year 2000 coming from Dr. Fritz had a lot more weight. I became excited.

"Could the big change that Dr. Fritz is predicting be something like the mass destruction of the planet Earth?"

"Dr. Fritz doesn't want to use the expression 'Armageddon' or call it an apocalyptic end of the world, but he warns that mankind needs to open its heart to the possibility of a big change or transformation as soon as possible and to prepare for it."

"If we get lazy or ignore these preparations, what does he say will happen?"

"If we can't prepare our hearts quickly enough, then humankind might expect a miserable result."

"Wow! That's very alarming, don't you think?"

"Yes. Dr. Fritz is not optimistic about this. Right now, humans are still fighting and making war, and, especially, we are polluting the planet pretty badly. At this point, he is not satisfied with human evolution at all. But while he is on this planet, the only thing he can do is to do his best. That's why he's working like crazy, trying to heal as many people's souls as he can."

As I listened to David, I felt I was facing something incredibly huge. At first, I was just curious about this psychic surgeon who did operations without anesthesia. Now we were talking about the future of humanity. And that future wasn't a million years later, but four years away. David said he intentionally didn't include this information in his video. Did that mean it might be better not to touch on this subject in this book? Readers might panic. And what responsibility did I have for them? If I delivered such a message, people might misunderstand the Dr. Fritz phenomenon. Maybe they would think of him as just another cult leader or guru predicting the end of the world.

"Can we also understand this big change in the year 2000 as an opportunity to evolve?" I asked David.

"Dr. Fritz said there is still a possibility that, if mankind's consciousness changes quickly and dramatically, the level of global consciousness can be raised. And the transformation that he is talking about isn't only about consciousness, but about evolution at the molecular level, also."

"You mean a change or evolution of the DNA code or something like that?"

"I think so. Maki-san, have you ever read the book *Bringers of the Dawn*, by Barbara Marciniak?"

"Yes, of course. It's become very popular."

"In that book, the entity Barbara channeled talks about the evolution of the DNA code."

"Yes, I remember."

"Recently, Dr. Eleanor Luzes visited Dr. Fritz and asked him about the content of *Bringers of the Dawn*. Dr. Fritz said that it was exactly right, but asked where she got that information."

"So that means there is the possibility of human evolution?"

"Yes. But I really can't imagine what percentage chance there is of it happening."

"Do you think that it's okay for me to write about this in my book?" I asked.

"I can't say anything about that. You must decide of your own free will, using your own judgment. But for me, I just decided to give you all the information I have about Dr. Fritz. Dr. Fritz called the year 2000 'the last exam for humankind,' and in order to pass that exam, we need to start an intensive study at the soul level as soon as possible."

"Whew! I didn't expect to have this kind of conversation! Do you have any other documents about this issue?"

"I was expecting you to ask," he said. "Actually, I have a very shocking interview I did with Dr. Fritz two years ago. It was in Portuguese, but for you, I translated it into seventeen pages of English. I couldn't help you with your research this time, or at least not as much as I wanted to, because I was so busy, so I'll give this to you as a souvenir of your visit."

As he said this, David removed a bunch of printed pages from his bag. From corner to corner, each page was full of typed English words. The title read, "Dr. Fritz through Rubens interview, Aug. 6, 1994."

I was overwhelmed with gratitude for his kindness, and, though I felt a little shy, I hugged him hard and thanked him from the depth of my heart. David's wife, Anna, appeared and told us that dinner was ready, so we moved into the dining room. Anna set the table and David gathered the four chairs from the other room. It was a simple dinner of spaghetti and eggplant, but their warmth and hospitality was tangible, and the spaghetti was especially delicious.

Over dinner, we talked about Christmas and the latest movies, not the year 2000. When the time came for us to leave so we could get ready for our flight home, it was really hard to say good-bye. David walked us to the gate of the apartment building and pointed to the middle of the apartment building next door. "The third one on the left on that floor is Rubens' home. It's got a pretty good view, too." Of course, at this time, Rubens would be treating hundreds of patients at the clinic. As I stood looking at his apartment, I thought how nice it would be if I could treat him to a one-week vacation in Japan.

Our airplane departed at eleven that evening. We checked in late, so Kaori and I were seated far apart. I was still full from the eggplant spaghetti, so instead of the in-flight dinner, I opted for a glass of red wine. Usually, when returning home from a trip, I like to think back over the experience and feel sentimental about it. But this time, my greatest desire was to read David's two-year-old interview with Dr. Fritz. Just as I took the pages out of the bag, the in-flight movie began. It was *Independence Day*, the blockbuster movie about an outer space attack on earth. I had already seen it in the theater. The similarity between its theme and the interview I was about to read made me smile.

Sitting and watching the movie's opening scenes without my earphones, I thought, "This movie is completely fictional, but can I dismiss Dr. Fritz's message as just fiction or, worse yet, bullshit?" As I read the interview, I began to tremble. It really got to me. Some of the interview repeated what David had told me that afternoon, but as I read further, recalling Dr. Fritz's voice and face, his words became more raw and real to me.

David had interviewed Dr. Fritz with the intent of developing a scenario for his film about the life of Arigó. Though David had researched Arigó's life, he had several questions that remained unanswered. Since Dr. Fritz used to manifest through Arigó, David directed his questions to Dr. Fritz. Although it had been twenty-five years since Arigó's death, Dr. Fritz, channeling through Rubens, recalled a lot about Arigó's life. For the next few pages I will simply quote some highlights from David's interview, without interjecting my own thoughts or feelings.

August 6, 1994

D: Dr. Fritz, these questions are about your experience with Arigó. I'd first like to ask, why was he selected as a medium?

F: Arigó?

D: Yes, Arigó.

F: Arigó, Edson Queiroz, Rubens, all of them have been part of my life. They are now paying for what they did. It is the opportunity they were given to be rescued. The form that this takes today is working, operating. I wasn't born only as Fritz. I was born before, also.

D: In this sense, you were also selected to work as Dr. Fritz?

F: Yes. The way he found was to put me into the war being a doctor, and that's what I had to work at. This way, getting to know the pain of war, I had the opportunity to get to know love. Because of this, I had to change, to work in this way, to be able to save others that I had been before and before and before. Not as me, not like I am.

D: Did you have any feeling, emotion, when you were selected to work with Arigó?

F: When I met Arigó, it wasn't an emotion. It was shock, because I had to work. Surprise.

D: Why surprise?

F: I didn't imagine I would have to return like that, working. I thought that had stopped, that I wouldn't have to return.

D: How old was he at that time?

F: He started the work in his town very early. In your human-being age, he was twenty.

D: Why did he die when he did, in a car accident?

F: My way of dying must be violent, not calm. It must be a fast way to die.

D: Why is that?

F: The way that they all have to die must be sudden, because not one of them can wait for their death lying in bed thinking that I helped so many others. They have to die quickly. None of them were weak, dying little by little. As the mediums progress, they get higher in spirit. So if they were to get sick and deteriorate over a long period of time, they would start to complain. But I don't want that level of soul to come down when they complain they are suffering on the bed. That's why they need to die all of a sudden, so I can retrieve their soul to join us.

D: The technique Rubens uses to treat patients is different now than in the days of Arigó. Why is that?

F: Now I cure, have them come two, three, four times. They could be cured on the first time, but I tell them to come four times. Faith accompanies, faith stimulates. He passes to her, to her, to her, increasing faith. As we have so little time now—and the mission isn't mine, but everyone's— the question of faith must be taken up. So the way to work can be quicker, less painful, less theatrical, but with the same effect, and with a greater effect of distributing faith and preparing all of your spirits.

D: What do you mean by "we have so little time?"

F: I have been learning for so many years on this planet, and I will learn more, and in six years I will go away and learn more in another place.

D: Did you or he have the ability to see the future of a person through their karma or spiritual energy, to tell if they had a chance to recover or if they were going to die?

F: Yes.

D: And how does this fit in with free will, compared with having a predestined path, when you have this preview of their future? [Dr. Fritz's assistant translates the question from Portuguese into German so that Dr. Fritz can better understand].

F: I can tell when that person will die. In that case, the most I can do is take care of them because they have pain, so that they can have a good moment, and they go away in peace. To not feel pain is no miracle. To not bleed is no miracle. A miracle is when you understand faith and distribute this, pass it forward. That's a miracle. I told Arigó what would happen with his death, and I told Edson Queiroz, and I'm going to tell Rubens what will happen and what the work will be and where the work will go.

D: What is the motive and goal of universal force?

F: Six years from now there will be a big change. If you don't get ready for these six years... It's not just me who does this. Others do too... If you don't get ready within six years, and well-prepared, very little will be left. If what is left over is not well-created, well-based, a great force that transmutes this will not be able to transmute it again to a better state, and then it will be dark again.

D: So the goal of this force is to be dark again?

F: Yes. Because of this there are so many people and channelers who operate, cure, working other ways, speak, write.

D: Is anyone doing film?

F: It has to be here. We have six years. So how do we change? We change with noise, blast, impacting force. When I hit [smacks his hand], few will be left. These few who are left are the ones who must learn. They will only learn when they transmit faith. Their child is cured, they tell someone else who tells someone else. And in this way, yes, they learn. So I continue to cut, they get better, they leave. But if I don't transmit faith, my work is worth nothing during all these years.

D: So what is actually going to happen in six years?

F: Now what's going to happen is that there is no other way out. Only six years, that's it. Boom!

D: Boom?

F: Boom! Yeah, boom! And if you don't learn now—those

who are good, learned. Those who stay, didn't learn. But you have to have the opportunity to change, to learn, to improve, and it hurts a bit.

D: So the work is going to be done, now that we are coming to the third millennium, huh?

F: In six years, it's going to change, so we must prepare now.

D: So the plan for me to make a feature film about Arigó/Dr. Fritz, is that one of the preparations?

F: Yes it is. That's what's important. You have to have love in the heart and understand that you are not just making a film but perpetuating ideas.

D: What is the reason you showed up in Brazil? This is my last question.

F: My manifestation here in Brazil is exactly because of the big noise that will happen.

D: Noise?

F: Noise. Boom! That will happen in six years.

Only six more years and "boom"! This might strike the reader as being kind of histrionic, but at the time of David's interview, the year 2000 was six years away. By the time you read this in America, there will be less than two years to go.

In the beginning of this book, I mentioned that I have made an effort not to think about negative apocalyptic predictions about the end of the century. I believed that books about Nostradamus and Armageddon were not supported by scientific evidence, that they were most likely sensational fiction written to sell books to people who read tabloids.

In fact, the last two Japanese books Kaori and I wrote earned us the nickname "gurubusters." In the first book, *Spiritual Adventures of a Sushi Chef*, we debunked an Indian prophecy scam that had become very popular in Japan. In the second book, we debunked a fake shaman in Peru who had ambitions of posing as a guru and messenger of the Incas to deceive gullible people in the United States and Japan.

So if our mission was the same here, it would be as gurubusters to debunk Dr. Fritz's fake treatments and predictions. But since I have to admit that his treatments are incredibly effective in curing thousands of patients, I can't just ignore the rest of what he says.

I never imagined I would end up writing a book with a scary prediction about the millennium. It wasn't my intention to sprinkle gasoline onto the fire of end-of-the-century paranoia. My research into the Dr. Fritz phenomenon simply led me to these prophecies. After witnessing so many of Dr. Fritz's miraculous operations and healings, I can't just dismiss his prophecy as a joke or fantasy.

I struggled for a long time over whether or not to pass along the content of the interview above. The last time I visited Japan, a high school friend invited me to dinner with his family. During the meal, he said to his daughter, who was in junior high school, "Your high school entrance exam is coming up soon, so you have to study harder and harder, right?" His daughter looked at him and yelled, "But, Daddy, the world is coming to an end in four years. I read it in the predictions of Nostradamus. If that's so, it's better to play as much as I can instead of studying and suffering."

I became so angry when I heard this that I wanted to hit the author of such stupid predictions. When I recall those emotions, I feel guilty, because now it is me spreading such ideas. I need to explain why I disclosed the contents of the interview with Dr. Fritz: His message had the kind of energy about it that demanded that I deliver it to other people. If the universe had arranged for me to meet Dr. Fritz in the way it did, then it seems to be my mission to deliver all of his message. So whether his message is to be taken seriously or ignored as bullshit, I leave totally to the perception and intuition of the reader.

At least I have done the job of delivering the message I was contracted to deliver, though my motivations may be frowned upon. You may wonder how I felt when I read this interview with Dr. Fritz. From here to the last line of this book, I have transcribed the notes exactly as I scribbled them on the airplane. Again, I feel a little ashamed of them, because I was far from calm, but I want to share my feelings exactly as they transpired. Here are the notes:

Right after I read this interview, I was overwhelmed. I couldn't control my excitement. Ironically, on the movie screen, the climactic battle between a gigantic UFO and a supersonic jet was taking place. I felt dismayed and panicked. Trying to act normal, I got up, walked to the back of the plane, and woke Kaori from her nap. She read the interview. Then her face turned red. She thought seriously for a few minutes, then looked as though she had come to an important decision. "Maki-san, I am going to totally change my lifestyle for the next four years."

"How?" I asked.

"I was going to buy a house with a thirty-year loan. But now, with that money, I am going to travel wherever I want to go, and do whatever I like to do at the moment."

"So if you spend all your savings and nothing happens in the year 2000, what are you going to do?"

After a pause, she said, "Well, then we'll have a big celebration."

"That's a great idea. A huge party!"

As we talked, I began to feel a lot easier and lighter. I thought, "Yes, it isn't necessary to be seriously depressed. I might not even make it to the year 2000. If I'm lucky, I might die tomorrow in a traffic accident. So, until then, like Dr. Moura told us in Ipanema, 'think with our hearts, feel with our hearts, and act with our hearts.' That's the way to go." Then, as Dr. Fritz told me, value every moment as precious and try to live like every day is the year 2000. Every day holds a big opportunity for a great transformation. And every day we can feel ultimate bliss.

So even if something terrible happens, this lifetime can be really lucky for us because we get to witness the biggest change in human history. We can live our lives fully until then, anyway. If I were told I had only one month to live because I had a terminal disease, then I couldn't do anything except suffer in a hospital bed for that month. But right now I'm fortunate to have such a healthy body and mind. So for four more years, I can eat whatever I like to eat and do whatever I like to do. Meanwhile, my soul can grow and mature for four more years. That is a thousand times better than living without any purpose and complaining every day.

In case the day of the big change really comes, I'd like to

reserve the best seats. And it would be really nice if I had some person I love next to me, hugging and holding me. Then we can have the biggest, most spectacular show in history. It will be great entertainment. And if nothing happens in the year 2000, then we are going to yell that Dr. Fritz is a big liar and open up the Dom Perignon and I'm going to kiss everyone around me.

Then, if you want to say, "Maki-san, you wrote a book about a fake!" and want to hit me, please do so. I would love to take it. Anyway, everyone has to die somehow, someday, and I totally believe that our souls go on forever, so there's nothing to lose. When I think this way, the air in my lungs begins to taste so sweet, and I feel compassion and love for everything around me. Even in this dark room in the airplane, where most of the people are asleep, I feel like everything is alive, and shining, and beautiful.

Yes, my friends, how lucky we are to be born on this wonderful planet in this wonderful era.

Afterword

By Stephen Larsen

Masao Maki is one of those astonishing individuals who seem able to slip in and out of the cracks in the visible world. I think of the "Clever Men" of Australia, who walk or fly the songlines, those mysterious conduits of psychic energy that unite geographical places, that are holy centers in the aboriginal landscape, acupuncture points connected by the mysterious invisible meridians that underlie the visible world.

It was along one of those meridians that Maki-san first moved into my awareness. My wife, Robin, and my son, Merlin, and I were planning a massive undertaking in the Amazon—a journey following the 1996 International Transpersonal Association Conference. Originally we had planned to bring thirty professionals to Mapia, a visionary community in the Rio Branco district of the Amazon. But the response to the "Wisdom of the Serpent Tour" had been overwhelming; we had over forty registrants and more requests arriving all the time. It seemed impossible to anticipate all the logistics. From Manaus, a rubber-trading town in the Amazon, we would all have to take two plane journeys over a distance of 1,000 miles—first on a jet and then a prop—then boat up the Rio Branco, and finally canoe by dugout up the Igarape Mapia; the last leg alone would take thirteen hours.

Now, having already tried several times to close registration, only to be sought out by another enthusiastic would-be participant, I was speaking to a nice Japanese man, who explained he was a writer and researcher. I very much liked and resonated with Maki-san, and wanted to make an exception, even though we had turned down many. But uncharacteristically, I found myself saying

"No." I am very sensitive to people's feelings and could sense his disappointment. But he was very gracious, saying he hoped we would meet in Manaus anyway. It was not until I read the manuscript of this remarkable book that I understood my "no" and began to glimpse the exquisite tangle of synchronicities that wove and unwove themselves along these particular songlines, working out an as yet unknown destiny for us all.

During the Manaus conference, made up of hundreds of people who had traveled from all over the world, I arranged for participants to be exposed to two large Santo Daime ceremonies. The followers of the Santo Daime Amazonian religion drink a sacred tea called ayahuasco (a mixture of the banisteriopsis vine and the leafy plant psychotriya viridis.) It is prepared in a highly ceremonial way, with prayer and ritual woven in. I had participated in Daime ceremonies, or "works," a number of times myself already, and had made arrangements with the conference such that some works might be made (unofficially) available to some of the conference participants.

During the ceremony, in a little rural temple outside Manaus, in which well over two hundred people drank the sacred tea and sang hymns channeled from the Astral World by the founders of the tradition, I suddenly became aware of the presence of two Japanese men behind me. It is for good reason that the first Europeans called ayahuasco "telepathine." As the tea surges through the veins, the mind opens like a flower with luminous petals. Surrounded by similar flowers, petals intermingling, one sometimes gets lost in regards to "whose mind is whose."

I addressed them in a whisper, in Japanese, before I learned that one of them spoke English beautifully. There, in the swirling mind-forms that come with the Daime—phosphorescent anacondas and jaguars—I sensed his amazing being. I met Masao Maki in the collective unconscious! Next to me was an old acquaintance, Dr. Arnie Mindell, who was drinking the sacred tea for the first time. My friend Dr. Rich Yensen was on the other side, trying somehow to capture the uncapturable with camera and recorder.

Strangers and friends alike, we were brothers with swirling

luminous indistinct boundaries. The wounds in my brothers' souls were my own; their glimpses of paradise were my own. (Men and women are segregated on either side of the church in Santo Daime ceremonies.) I felt Maki and his friend's amazement at the visionary opening occurring inside themselves. Terence McKenna says the main danger of the DMT experience is "death by astonishment," but I felt these men's wounds and loves as if I had known them for years.

I also met David Sonnenschein at the conference in Manaus. He told me he had read my book *The Shaman's Doorway*, first published in 1975, and knew I had a penchant for the miraculous. I had learned of the Dr. Fritz phenomenon from the book *Arigo of the Rusty Knife* and through Dr. Stanley Krippner, an old friend and mentor, who also pursues the miraculous wherever he finds it. With lots of other conference participants, I was able to witness David's mind-boggling film about Dr. Fritz and have some good conversations with him. He invited me to look him up in Rio de Janeiro when our group arrived.

The amazing conference ended, and our Amazonian journey began to unfold, with its own trials and healings. A week or so later, our group of American and European pilgrims emerged from the jungle, shaken, but confirmed in the richness and integrity of a perilous adventure undertaken together and in the presence of divine support and synchronous connections on every hand. We now went on to what seemed like the "fleshpots" of Rio for the last phase.

One of our culminating events was to experience a Daime works in Rio's urban center, but the main *padrinho*, Paolo Roberto, was out of town. Only a few of us went to the works, and many were disappointed at the loss of our journey's culminating event. I asked the group if they would like to make an unscheduled visit to Dr. Fritz, and the result was a resounding "Yes!"

When I called David, he was immediately responsive, and set up a special arrangement for our entire group to watch Dr. Fritz at work. In a large bus, we drove through a squalid section of Rio to what seemed to be an abandoned warehouse. The songline led us through the littered sidewalk, past the vendors clustered around the entrance and exit of the warehouse, through the dilapidated building, and suddenly face to face with Maki-san, who had been in Rio studying Dr. Fritz all the time that we were in the Amazon. It was a joyful reunion, as we swapped stories of miracles. I invited Maki to join us for dinner the following evening with David, his family, and one of our participants who would stay on in Rio, Dr. Jeremy Waletsky.

On our tour were twelve MDs, an equal number of Ph.D.s, several clinical social workers and CEOs of corporations—not your average group of tourists, nor very gullible. We were led in to Dr. Fritz about five at a time. In my own small group were several American physicians, who wanted to watch Dr. Fritz as closely as possible. A large French film crew was just finishing its work of capturing Dr. Fritz in action.

Only once before, in India twenty years previous, had anyone spoken to me inside my mind. I had been traveling with my wife and small child through a difficult area. I had to find our contact, who had a car waiting, while my wife and child sat with the luggage. A large and unruly crowd were besieging us. A tall, magnificent Tantrika spoke in my mind, clearly saying, "Go, I will protect them for you!" And he did, magnificently. My wife reported he hovered above them like a lion, sending the beggars and thieves cowering away. I was eternally grateful to that man, and boggled by what had happened.

Now Dr. Fritz seemed to be speaking in my mind. (It seems strange to recount this, but at the time it seemed normal.) "Hello, I know who you are and what you do. Delighted to meet you. May God bless your work." I felt like I had known him for a long time, as I simultaneously felt somehow known by him. Over the next few minutes, I heard him speak fluent English, French, and German to various people (Rubens Faria, as far as I know, is fluent only in Portuguese). Dr. Fritz moved in a kind of blur, and we were privileged to watch him wield his scalpel and scissors with amazing deftness, opening people up and removing things. He motioned some of our doctors to watch him very closely, which they were eager to do. The atmosphere was indescribable.

My wife Robin was traveling with another group. Dr. Fritz also seemed to speak in her mind, she later recalled. "Are you ready?" he asked her. He seemed to know about and to be referring to her blind left eye, damaged at age seven, when a demented older child plunged a pair of scissors into it. "N-not yet" she indicated, unwilling to have another sharp object inserted into her eye. "Whenever you are…" he seemed to say, gently.

Immediately thereafter, he addressed Guilherme, our translator for the journey, in Portuguese. Guilherme indicated he was ready, and suddenly Dr. Fritz plunged the scalpel into his eye—which I believe suffered from astigmatism—and moved it around a little. Then he indicated to his assistants to bandage the eye. For the next twenty-four hours, Guilherme seemed to be in shock or a trance. He told me he was very tired, and he slept like a log that night. The following day he was able to remove the bandage and his vision was actually improved! It was still better when I talked to him several months later.

But another strange event happened. One of our participants, a CEO of a corporation, seemed to have her own ideas about everything. For example, I had tried to no avail to counsel her not to wear expensive jewelry so conspicuously in Rio because of the danger of being robbed. She had laughed the advice off. Now she emerged from her meeting with Dr. Fritz, weeping uncontrollably. I sat with her, offering comfort and support. Finally, when she was able to speak, she shared what had happened. "I felt as if I were in a roomful of angels, and I…I was so unworthy." For the rest of the trip we found ourselves with a gentler, humbler participant— open in a way that none of us had ever seen her. Dr. Fritz had not touched nor spoken to her, it was the atmosphere around him, she said, that worked this remarkable internal transformation.

After our tour dispersed, we spent the evening with David, his family, and Jeremy Waletsky. Maki describes the evening in this book. The spirits flowed freely, because we had all been on a very simple diet without alcohol for over a month. We waxed metaphysical about all we had seen and done. Thereafter, Robin and

Merlin and Jeremy and I traveled up the coast to Salvadore de Bahia to experience the ceremonies of Umbanda and Candomble. In Bahia, the African cultural and spiritual presence in Brazil is very evident. There we attended the legendary trance ceremonies in which spirits of the Orishas (the Yoruba gods) dressed as and acknowledged to embody a particular deity, mount some participants.

During this time of rest and recuperation, our twenty-seven-year-old son, Merlin, who had been injured in a climbing accident two years before, told us that when we returned to Rio preparatory to departure for the States, he would like to remain there and be treated by Dr. Fritz. He felt very strongly about this decision.

As his parents, we could not help but remind him that Dr. Fritz treats thousands of people at a time, not always with sterilized implements, and that it was not unlikely that among those patients were many AIDS and HIV-positive people. Our parental hearts also had misgivings about a young crippled *Yanqui* at large in Rio—where he might be easy prey for muggers.

But Merlin, a very active young man and a professional mountain climbing guide, had spent much of the past two years in a wheelchair, and had undergone three operations at the New York Hospital for Special Surgery. But still he was in pain—bone spurs kept growing out of the cracks in his shattered heel—and all through our journey in the Amazon he, our EMT (emergency medical technician), had traveled on crutches. He felt terribly limited and was determined to try Dr. Fritz's healing. He would be accompanied by Jeremy, a friend we trusted very much. So we changed his ticket and anxiously boarded our plane for the States.

Dr. Fritz was extraordinarily kind and sweet to our son when he came for treatment a couple of days later. He only gave him an injection that day but told Merlin to return the following day for an operation.

Once again he was warmly welcomed and asked if he felt ready. Merlin said "Yes." Jeremy was allowed to watch from only a foot or two away. Merlin said all doubt about sleight-of-hand or other tricks vanished when the scalpel went in. Pain was present, but somehow bearable. It was a real, palpable experience, as the deftly wielded knife trimmed the bone spurs. Within a very few moments the astonishing process was over. Jeremy saw the wound bleeding freely. Then Dr. Fritz went down the wound—nip, nip, nip with his fingers—except that there was no suturing material in his hand. The wound closed up save for an oozing drop of blood—nip! Dr. Fritz motioned to the attendants to bind the wound and looked sternly at Merlin. "Stay off it for six hours!" He was done.

Merlin left on his crutches. That night he experienced a close call. He was almost mugged on the streets of Rio, but managed to slip out of the situation. The next day he awakened feeling "uncommonly good." He decided to go and see one of the famous rock-climbing areas in the city. There were a number of climbers on the imposing granite cliff, and as he watched, one of them hailed him: "Yanqui—you want to tie in?" (To "tie in" means to be put on a roped belay for safety.) "I only have sneakers with me, and I've just had an operation," Merlin said, indicating his bandaged foot. "Aw, come on, Yanqui. Just try something easy."

Merlin has never been able to turn down an opportunity to climb. He tied into the rope and went easily up the climb they put him on. Then they put him on a harder one. Eventually he climbed the hardest climbs on the cliff (5.11 to 5.12 in the U.S. system) with his bandaged foot. When the climbers learned he had just been to Dr. Fritz the previous day and was climbing like that already, he became a celebrity.

A week later, Merlin returned to the States, still on crutches. He told us the story—to our great amazement—and showed us the still obvious scar on his heel where the scalpel had gone in. It was about three inches long and there were no suture marks on the pinkish lips of the wound. It was obviously healing well and looked like the work of an expert surgeon. A few days after returning home, Merlin put his crutches away for good. "I'm not going to use these anymore," he said. He has noticed that since the "psychic surgery" his energy is much better: he feels more alert, is a little better organized, and has a better attitude.

A few months ago I watched Merlin bound joyfully through the woods during a hike, in no apparent pain. He walks up to five miles, loaded with ropes and heavy climbing equipment. Early last winter (1997) he participated in the Empire State Games, New York's statewide Olympics, as a competitor in judo, and fought many difficult matches, placing very high (fourth) in his division. As of the date of this writing, June 1998, just exactly two years after our miracle-filled Brazilian trip, he still has some problems when his foot is in an awkward position for a long time, like on the steep roof we just put on his house. He is thinking of making another trip to see Dr. Fritz, which we may realize this fall.

I waited awhile after receiving Masao Maki's manuscript before reading it, because of all the complex feelings I thought it might bring up in me. But once I started, I couldn't put it down till I was finished! This is an extraordinary book by an extraordinary man about events that constantly push our envelope.

Masao Maki was, by his own account, a little like the biblical Saul on the road to Emmaeus; Maki's goal was to debunk psychic fraud, wherever it could be found. Perhaps in this way he was the ideal candidate for the synchronous experiences that befell him, beginning with the unexpected airport prophecy that he would meet someone named Dr. Fritz. Maki found he was moving along webs of the miraculous. All he could do was remain open and let himself be led. In the presence of authentic miracles he became a convert to the idea of the miraculous.

Maki has the versatility of a Renaissance man: journalist, writer, musician, sushi chef, business owner. Bilingual and bicultural, he seems the ideal "traveler in many worlds," moving easily from one cultural zone to another along the songlines that he has now discovered lead from one destination of the soul to another.

If I hadn't said no to Maki, and he had joined our tour, there is no doubt that he still would have been exposed to the miraculous—for it seems we all moved amidst constant miracles in the spirit-imbued world of Brazilian culture. (The book explains a little of the "why" of this from the perspective of Dr. Fritz's spirits.) But Maki needed to be on his own journey, to develop his unique relationship to the culture and world of possibilities that awaited him. Otherwise, he might not have gotten initiated so deeply into the Dr. Fritz phenomenon, and this book probably would not have been written

This book is honest, carefully researched, and truthful in every aspect I have looked into. In this respect it was very interesting to read in Maki's account another side of the same unusual events I experienced, and to see just how he moved along meridians parallel to the ones we were on. Maki has done his job well, researching the origins of the traditions and healers he encountered. Maki's writing is remarkably good, and very accessible. One can feel Maki's integrity in his writing; he includes an honest self-portrait in the narrative, so we feel like we are traveling with a familiar and beloved companion.

If you wish to learn more about an authentic miracle alive in our time, read this book. From Castaneda and Don Juan to Kyriakos Markides and Daskalos, the quest goes on. There is a new genre, of which this book is a fine example, in which the most enterprising souls on our planet go in search of the ancient wisdom from which the miraculous emerges. Dr. Fritz, whether he be the disembodied spirit of a German doctor or a throng of angelic physicians, gives Maki a message recognizable from the perennial philosophy: love one another, cultivate understanding and compassion in all things, refine your sense of gratitude, pray deeply for the well-being of the planet. If you can do so, the miraculous will flood your life.

Dr. Fritz
Healing the Body and Spirit

A Documentary by David Sonnenschein
(90 minutes, NTSC, English version, 1996)

The phenomenon of channeled healing in Brazil through the German spirit Dr. Fritz began almost fifty years ago with the medium Zé Arigó and continues today with engineer Rubens Faria, who treats more than a thousand people a day in Rio de Janeiro suffering from diseases ranging from cataracts and arthritis to cancer and brain tumors. More fascinating than these remarkable cures is the fact that these patients receive no anesthesia yet feel no pain. In addition, the surgical instruments are not sterilized, yet a case of infection has never been recorded in over a decade of treatments.

This documentary penetrates the story of Rubens and Dr. Fritz, examining what Dr. Fritz does, how this is explained by psychologists and scientists, and why he has made himself available to aid in the spiritual evolution of the planet. Rubens tells about his childhood and how he first incorporated Dr. Fritz. This portrayal of the relationship between Rubens and Dr. Fritz is an example of an extraordinary collaboration between the physical and spiritual worlds that reveals how people go in and out of the trance state, what the different levels of consciousness are, and what kind of agreement they have to be able to work together.

Invited specialists including Stanley Krippner, Stephen Larsen, and Arny Mindell give their viewpoints in the areas of parapsychology, energy medicine, quantum physics, spirituality, and mythology. Rubens personal life is described by his mother, sister, and wife. Besides healing, Dr. Fritz participates in brainwave research and teaches a course training people to control energy in their astral bodies.

This documentary was inspired by the research for a feature film about the life of Zé Arigó by American filmmaker David Sonnenschein, who has lived in Brazil for the last decade. Besides his experience in film and television, Mr. Sonnenschein also practices the healing art of Kiatsu, using the principles of Aikido and Ki energy. This video is a coproduction of his production company, Crystal Vision, with Sergio Sztancsa ("Alemão") of Christal Produces.

For more information, contact David Sonnenschein at crystal@ax.apc.org or by telephone/fax (Brazil) 011 (5521) 326-1513.